A Short History of France

Parmele Mary Platt

Contents

A SHORT HISTORY
OF FRANCE

BY

Parmele Mary Platt

A SHORT HISTORY OF FRANCE.

CHAPTER I.

ONE of the greatest achievements of modern research is the discovery of a key by which we may determine the kinship of nations. What we used to conjecture, we now know. An identity in the structural form of language establishes with scientific certitude that however diverse their character and civilizations, Russian, German, Englishman, Frenchman, Spaniard, are all but branches from the same parent stem, are all alike children of the Asiatic Aryan.

So skilful are modern methods of questioning the past, and so determined the effort to find out its secrets, we may yet know the origin and history of this wonderful Asiatic people, and when and why they left their native continent and colonized upon the northern shores of the Mediterranean. Certain it is, however, that, more centuries before the Christian era than there have been since, they had peopled Western Europe.

This branch of the Aryan family is known as the Keltic, and was older brother to the Teuton and Slav, which at a much later period followed them from the ancestral home, and appropriated the middle and eastern portions of the European Continent.

The name of Gaul was given to the territory lying between the Ocean and the Mediterranean, and the Pyrenees and the Alps. And at a later period a portion of Northern Gaul, and the islands lying north of it, received from an invading chieftain and his tribe the name **Brit** or **Britain** (or Pryd or Prydain).

If the mind could be carried back on the track of time, and we could see what we now call France as it existed twenty centuries before the Christian era, we should behold the same natural features: the same mountains rearing their heads; the same rivers flowing to the sea; the same plains stretching out in the sunlight. But instead of vines and flowers and cultivated fields we should behold great herds of wild ox and elk, and of swine as fierce as wolves, ranging in a climate as cold as Norway; and vast, inaccessible forests, the home of beasts of prey, which contended with man for food and shelter.

Let us read Guizot's description of life in Gaul five centuries before Christ:

"Here lived six or seven millions of men a bestial life, in dwellings dark and low, built of wood and clay and covered with branches or straw, open to daylight by the door alone and confusedly heaped together behind a rampart of timber, earth, and stone, which enclosed and protected what they were pleased to call—a *town.*"

Such was the Paris and such the Frenchmen of the age of Pericles! And the same tides that washed the sands of Southern Gaul, a few hours later ebbed and flowed upon the shores of Greece—rich in culture, with refinements and subtleties in art which are the despair of the world to-day—with an intellectual endowment never since attained by any people.

The same sun which rose upon temples and palaces and life serene and beautiful in Greece, an hour later lighted sacrificial altars and hideous orgies in the forests of Gaul. While the Gaul was nailing the heads of human victims to his door, or hanging them from the bridle of his horse, or burning or flogging his prisoners to death, the Greek, with a literature, an art, and a civilization in ripest perfection, discussed with his friends the deepest problems of life and destiny, which were then baffling human intelligence, even as they are with us today. Truly we of Keltic and Teuton descent are late-comers upon the stage of national life.

There was no promise of greatness in ancient Gaul. It was a great, unregulated force, rushing hither and thither. Impelled by insatiate greed for the possessions of their neighbors, there was no permanence in their loves or their hatreds. The enemies of to-day were the allies of to-morrow. Guided entirely by the fleeting desires and passions of the moment, with no far-reaching plans to restrain, the sixty or more tribes composing the Gallic people were in perpetual state of feud and anarchy, apparently insensible to the ties of brotherhood, which give concert of action, and stability in form of national life. If they overran a neighboring country, it seemed not so much for permanent acquisition, as to make it a camping-ground until its resources were exhausted.

We read of one Massillia who came with a colony of Greeks long ages ago, and after founding the city of Marseilles, created a narrow, bright border of Greek civilization along the southern edge of the benighted land. It was a brief illumination, lasting only a century or more, and leaving few traces; but it may account for the superior intellectual quality which later distinguished Provence, the home of minstrelsy.

It requires a vast extent of territory to sustain a people living by the chase, and upon herds and flocks; hence the area which now amply maintains forty millions of Frenchmen was all too small for six or seven million Gauls; and they were in perpetual struggle with their neighbors for land—more land.

"Give us land," they said to the Romans, and when land was denied them and the gates of cities disdainfully closed upon their messengers, not land, but vengeance, was their cry; and hordes of half-naked barbarians trampled down the vineyards, and rushed, a tumultuous torrent, upon Rome.

The Romans could not stand before this new and strange kind of warfare. The Gauls streamed over the vanquished legions into the Eternal City, silent and deserted save only by the Senate and a few who remained intrenched in the Citadel; and there the barbarians kept them besieged for seven months, while they made themselves at home amid uncomprehended luxuries.

Of course Roman skill and courage at last dislodged and drove them back. But the fact remained that the Gaul had been there—master of Rome; that the iron-clad legions had been no match for his naked force, and a new sensation thrilled through the length and breadth of Gaul. It was the first throb of national life. The sixty or more fragments drew closer together into something like Gallic unity—with a common danger to meet, a common foe to drive back.

Hereafter there was another hunger to be appeased besides that for food and land; a hunger for conquest, for vengeance, and for glory for the Gallic name. National pride was born.

For years they hovered like wolves about Rome. But skill and superior intelligence tell in the centuries. It took long—and cost no end of blood and treasure; but two hundred years from the capture of Rome, the Gauls were driven out of Italy, and the Alps pronounced a barrier set by nature herself against barbarian encroachments.

Italy was not the only country suffering from the destroying footsteps of the Western Kelts. There had been long before an overflow of a tribe in Northern Gaul (the Kymrians), which had hewed and plundered its way south and eastward; until at the time of Alexander (B.C. 340) it was knocking at the gates of Macedonia.

Stimulated by the success at Rome fifty years earlier, they were, with fresh insolence, demanding "land," and during the centuries which followed, the Gallic name acquired no fresh lustre in Greece. Half-naked, gross, ferocious, and ignorant, sometimes allies, but always a scourge, they finally crossed the Hellespont (B.C. 278), and turned their attention to Asia Minor. And there, at last, we find them settled in a province called Gallicia, where they lived without amalgamating with the people about them, and four hundred years after Christ were speaking the language of their tribal home in what is now Belgium. And these were the Galatians— the "foolish Galatians," to whom Paul addressed his epistle; and we have followed up this Gallic thread simply because it mingles with the larger strand of ancient and sacred history with which we are all so familiar.

It is not strange that Roman courage became a byword. The fibre of Rome was toughened by perpetual strain of conflict. Even while she was struggling with Gaul and with the memories of the Carthaginian wars still fresh at Rome, the Goths were at her gates—their blows directed with a solidity superior to that of the barbarians who had preceded them. Where the Gauls had knocked, the Goths thundered.

Again the city was invaded by barbarian feet, and again did superior training and intelligence drive back the invading torrent and triumph over native brute force.

Such, in brief outline, was the condition of the centuries just before the Christian era.

It is easy now to read the meaning of these agitated centuries, and to recognize the preparation for the passing of the old and the coming of the new.

CHAPTER II.

THE making of a nation is not unlike bread or cake making. One element is used as the basis, to which are added other component parts, of varying qualities, and the result we call England, or Germany, or France. The steps by which it is accomplished, the blending and fusing of the elements, require centuries, and the process makes what we call—history.

It was written in the book of fate that Gaul should become a great nation; but not until fused and interpenetrated with two other nationalities. She must first be humanized and civilized by the Roman, and then energized and made free from the Roman by the Teuton.

The instrument chosen for the former was Julius Cæsar, and for the latter—five centuries later—Clovis, the Frankish leader.

It is safe to affirm that no man has ever so changed the course of human events as did Julius Cæsar. Napoleon, who strove to imitate him 1800 years later, was a charlatan in comparison; a mere scene-shifter on a great theatrical stage. Few traces of his work remain upon humanity to-day.

Cæsar opened up a pathway for the old civilizations of the world to flow into Western Europe, and the sodden mass of barbarism was infused with a life-compelling current. This was not accomplished by placing before the inferior race a higher ideal of life for imitation, but by a mingling of the blood of the nations—a transfusion into Gallic veins of the germs of a higher living and thinking—thus making them heirs to the great civilizations of antiquity.

Was any human event ever fraught with such consequences to the human race as the conquest of Gaul by Julius Cæsar?

The Gallic wars had for centuries drained the treasure and taxed the resources of Rome. Cæsar conceived the audacious idea of stopping them at their source—in fact, of making Gaul a Roman province.

It was a marvellous exhibition, not simply of force, but of force wielded by supreme intelligence and craft. He had lived many years among this people and knew their sources of weakness, their internal jealousies and rivalries, their incohesiveness. When they hurled themselves against Rome, it was as a mass of sharp fragments. When the Goths did the same, it was as one solid, indivisible body. Cæsar saw that by adroit management he could disintegrate this people while conquering them.

By forcibly maintaining in power those who submitted to him, being by turns gentle and severe, ingratiating here, terrifying there, he established a tremendous personal force; and during nine years carried on eight campaigns, marvels in the art of war, as well as in the subtler methods of negotiation and intrigue. He had successively dealt with all the Keltic tribes, even including Great Britain, subjugating either through their own rivalries, or by his invincible arm.

Equally able to charm and to terrify, he had all the gifts, all the means to success and empire, that can be possessed by man. Great in politics as in war, as full of resource in the forum as on the battle-field, he was by nature called to dominion.

It was not as a patriot, simply intent upon freeing Rome of an harassing enemy, that he endured those nine years in Gaul; not as a great leader burning with military ardor that he conducted those eight campaigns. The conquest of Gaul meant the greater conquest of Rome. The one was accomplished; he now turned his back upon the devastated country, and prepared to complete his great project of human ascendency.

Rome was mistress of the world; he—would be master of Rome.

In the early days of the conquest of Gaul a small island lying in the river Seine was chosen for the residence of the Roman Governors, and called *Lutetia.* The residence soon grew into the Palace of the Cæsars; and then bridges spanned the river, and roads and aqueducts and faubourgs sprang into existence across the Seine, and *Lutetia* was swallowed up in Paris—so named for a Gallic tribe, the *Parisii,* which had once encamped there. Standing within the Palais de Justice on this island to-day, one is in direct touch with Rome when she was mistress of the world. The feet of the Cæsars have pressed those stones. Those vaulted ceilings have looked down upon Julian the Apostate; he who upon his throne in the far East sighed for "Lutetia"—his "dear Lutetia."

At Passy and Montmartre, and where stands the Palais Royal, rich Romans had their suburban homes, and Roman legions were encamped where are now the Palais de Luxembourg and the Sorbonne. And with a mingling of Keltic and Latin, there had commenced a new form of human speech.

Not Paris alone, but all of Gaul felt the awakening touch of a great civilization, and with improved ideals in living there came another great advance. The human sacrifices and abhorrent practices of the Druidical faith were abandoned, and Jupiter and Minerva and the gods of Parnassus supplanted the grim deities of a more ancient mythology. But while Rome was a powerful teacher, she was a cruel mistress—and shackles were galling to these free barbarians. In the midst of universal misery there came tidings of something better than the gods of Parnassus, when in A.D. 160 Irenæus came to Lyons and there established the first Church of Christ; and here it was that Marcus Aurelius ordered the persecution which was intended to stamp out the new and fanatical heresy.

CHAPTER III.

WHILE the Star of Empire was thus moving toward the West, another and brighter star had arisen in the East. So accustomed are we to the story, that we lose all sense of wonder at its recital.

Julius Cæsar's brief triumph was over. Marc Antony had recited his virtues over his bier, Rome had wept, and then forgotten him in the absorbing splendors of his nephew Augustus. In an obscure village of an obscure country in Asia Minor the young wife of a peasant finds shelter in a stable, and gives birth to a son, who is cradled in the straw of a manger from which the cattle are feeding.

Can the mind conceive of human circumstances more lowly? The child grew to manhood, and in his thirty-three years of life was never lifted above the obscure sphere into which he was born; never spoke from the vantage-ground of worldly elevation; simply moving among people of his own station in life, mechanics, fishermen, and peasants, he told of a religion of love, a gospel of peace, for which he was willing to die.

Who would have dreamed that this was the germ of the most potent, the most regenerative force the world had ever known? That thrones, empires, principalities, and powers would melt and crumble before His name? Of all miracles, is not this the greatest?

The passionate ardor with which this religion was propagated in the first two centuries had no motive but the yearning to make others share in its benefits and hopes; and to this end to accept the belief that Jesus Christ had come in fulfilment of the promise of a Saviour—who should be sent to this world clothed with divine authority to establish a spiritual kingdom, in which he was King of kings, Lord of lords, Meditator between us and the Father, of whom he was the "only begotten Son."

The religion in its essence was absolutely simple. Its founder summed it up in two sentences: expressing the duty of man to man, and of man to God. That was all the theology he formulated.

For two centuries the religion of Christ was an elemental spiritual force. It appealed only to the highest attributes and longings of the human soul, and under its sustaining influence frail women, men, and even children were able to endure tortures, of which we cannot read even now without shuddering horror.

Nature's method of gardening is very beautiful. She carefully guards the seed until it is ripe, then she bursts the imprisoning walls and gives it to the winds to distribute. Precisely such method was used in disseminating Christianity. It was not for one people—it was for the healing of the nations, and its home was wherever man abides.

Nearly five decades after Christ's death upon the cross, Jerusalem was destroyed by Titus. The home of Christianity was effaced. At just the right moment the enclosing walls had broken, and freed to the winds the germs in all their primitive purity.

Imperial favor had not tarnished it, human ambitions had not employed and degraded it, nor had it been made into complex system by ingenious casuists. The pure spiritual truth, unsullied as it came from the hand of its founder, was scattered broadcast, as the band of Christians dispersed throughout the Roman Empire, naturally forming into communities here and there, which became the centres of Christian propagandism. Lyons in Gaul was such a centre.

The fires of persecution had been lighted here and there throughout the empire, and the Emperor Nero, under whom the Apostles Peter and Paul are said to have suffered martyrdom, had amused himself by making torches of the Christians at Rome. But until A.D. 177 Gaul was exempt from such horrors.

Marcus Aurelius—that peerless pagan—large in intelligence, exalted in character, and guided by a conscientious rectitude which has made his name shine like a star in the lurid light of Roman history, still failed utterly to comprehend the significance of this spiritual kingdom established by Christ on earth. He it was who ordered the first persecution in Gaul. In pursuance of his command, horrible tortures were inflicted at Lyons upon those who would not abjure the new faith.

A letter, written by an eye-witness, pictures with terrible vividness the scenes which followed. Many cases are described with harrowing detail, and of one Blandina it is said: "From morn till eve they put her to all manner of torture, marvelling that she still lived with her body pierced through and through and torn piecemeal by so many tortures, of which a single one should have sufficed to kill her; to which she only replied, 'I am a Christian' "

The recital goes on to tell how she was then cast into a dungeon—her feet compressed and dragged out to the utmost tension of the muscles—then left alone in darkness until new methods of torture could be devised.

Finally she was brought, with other Christians, into the amphitheatre, hanging from a cross to which she was tied, and there thrown to the beasts. As the beasts refused to touch her she was taken back to the dungeon to be reserved for another occasion, being brought out daily to witness the fate and suffering of her friends and fellow-martyrs; still answering the oft-repeated question, "I am a Christian."

The writer goes on to say, "After she had undergone fire, the talons of beasts, and every agony which could be thought of, she was wrapped in a network and thrown to a bull, who tossed her in the air"—and her sufferings were ended.

Truly it cost something to say "I am a Christian" in those days.

Marcus Aurelius probably gave orders for the persecution at Lyons, with little knowledge of what would be the nature of those persecutions, or of the religion he was trying to exterminate. Some of the hours spent in writing introspective essays would have been well employed in studying the period in which he lived, and the empire he ruled.

Paganism and Druidism, those twin monsters, receded before the advancing light of Christianity. Neither contained anything which could nourish the soul of man, and both had become simply badges of nationality.

Druidism was the last stronghold of independent Gallic life. It was a mixture of northern myth and oriental dreams of metempsychosis, coarse, mystical, and cruel. The Roman paganism which was superimposed by the conquering race was the mere shell of a once vital religion. Educated men had long ceased to believe in the gods and divinities of Greece, and it is said that the Roman augurs, while giving their solemn prophetic utterances, could not look at each other without laughing.

In the year 312—alas for Christianity!—it was espoused by imperial power. When the Emperor Constantine declared himself a Christian, there was no doubt rejoicing among the saints; but it was the beginning of the degeneracy of the religion of Christ. The faith of the humble was to be raised to a throne; its lowly garb to be exchanged for purple and scarlet; the gospel of peace to be enforced by the sword.

The empire was crumbling, and upon its ruins the race of the future and social conditions of modern times were forming. Paganism and Druidism would have been an impossibility. Christianity, even with its lustre dimmed, its purity tarnished, its simplicity overlaid with scholasticism, was better than these. The miracle had been accomplished. The great Roman Empire had said, "I am Christian."

A belief in the gods of Parnassus, which Rome had imposed upon Gaul, had now become a heresy to be exterminated. If fires were lighted at Lyons or elsewhere, they were for the extermination not of Christians, but of pagans, and of all who would depart from the religion of Christ as interpreted by Rome. It was a death-bed repentance for the cruel old empire, a repentance which might delay, but could not avert a calamitous ending, and an unexpected event was near at hand which would hasten the coming of the end.

It was in the year A.D. 375 that the Huns, a terrible race of beings, came out from that then mysterious but now historic region, lying between China and Russia, and surged into Europe under the leadership of Attila, sweeping before them as they came Goths, Vandals, and other Teutonic races, as if with a predetermined purpose of forcing the uncivilized Teuton into the lap of a perishing civilization in the south. Then having accomplished this, after the defeat of Attila at Châlons in A.D. 453, they disappeared forever as a race from the stage of human events.

This is the time when Paris was saved by Genevieve, the poor sheperdess, who, like an early Joan of Arc, awoke the people from the apathy of despair, and led them to victory—and is rewarded by an immortality as "Saint Genevieve," the patron saint of Paris. It would seem that the vigilance of the gentle saint has either slept or been unequal to the task of protecting her city at times!

It was the combined forces of the Goth and the Frank which drove this scourge out of Europe. Meroveus, or Meroveg, the leader of the Franks in this great achievement, once the terror of the Gallic people, was now their deliverer. He had won the gratitude of all classes, from bishops to slaves, throughout Gaul, and fate had thus opened wide a door leading into the future of that land.

CHAPTER IV.

GUAL had been Latinized and Christianized. Now one more thing was needed to prepare her for a great future. Her fibre was to be toughened by the infusion of a stronger race. Julius Cæsar had shaken her into submission, and Rome had chastised her into decency of behavior and speech, but as her manners improved her native vigor declined. She took kindly to Roman luxury and effeminacy, and could no longer have thundered at the gates of her neighbors demanding "land."

The despotism of a perishing Roman Empire had become intolerable; and the thoughts of an overtaxed and enslaved people turned naturally to the Franks. They had rescued them from one terrible fate, might they not deliver them from another? And so it came about that the young savage Chlodoveg, or *Clovis,* grandson of Meroveus, found himself master of the fair land long coveted beyond the Rhine; and Gaul and Roman alike were submerged beneath the Teuton flood, while Clovis, sitting in the Palace of the Cæsars, on the island in the Seine, was wearing the kingly crown, and independent and dynastic life had commenced in what was hereafter to be not Gaul, but *France.*

But the king of whom she had dreamed was of her own race; not this terrible Frank. Had she exchanged one servitude for another? Had she been, not set free, but simply annexed to the realm of the barbarian across the Rhine? Let us say rather that it was an espousal. She had brought her dowry of beauty and "land," that most coveted of possessions, and had pledged obedience, for which she was to be cherished, honored, and protected, and to bear the name of her lord.

It will be well not to examine too closely the conversion of Clovis to Christianity, any more than that of Constantine to the religion of Christ, or that of Henry VIII. to Protestantism. The only thing Clovis wanted of the gods was aid in destroying his enemies. At a certain dark moment, when the pagan deities failed him, and the tide of battle was turning against him, in desperation he offered to become a Christian, if the God of the Christians would save him. He kept his word. His victory was followed by Christian baptism, and the Church had won a great defender, whose ferocious instincts were thereafter to be directed toward the extermination of unbelievers. And while hewing and consolidating and bringing his kingdom into form, whether by treacheries or intrigues or assassination, this converted Frank was not alone defender of the faith, but of the orthodox faith. The Visigoth kingdom in Spain was given over to that heresy known as ***Arianism!*** So in a crusade, like another of a later date, he swept them over beyond the Pyrenees, thus establishing a frontier which always remained.

Such were the rough beginnings of France, geographically and historically.

Ancient heroes are said to be seen through a shadowy lens, which magnifies their stature. Let us hope that the crimes of the three or four generations immediately succeeding Clovis have been in like manner expanded; for it is sickening to read of such monstrous prodigality of wickedness; whole families butchered—husbands, wives, children, anything obstructing the path to the throne—with an atrocity which makes Richard III. seem a mere pigmy in the art of intrigue and killing. The chapter closes with the daughter and mother of kings (Brunhilde or Brunhaut), naked, and tied by one arm, one leg, and her hair to the tail of an unbroken horse, and amid jeers and shouts dashed over the stones of Paris (A.D. 600).

Upon the death of Clovis his inheritance was divided among four sons, who, with their wives and families and their tempestuous passions, afforded material for a great epic. Whether Fredegunde or Brunhilde was the more terrible who can say? But the story of these rival queens, with their loves and their hatreds and their ambitious, vengeful fury, is more like the story of demons than of women. But these conditions led to two results which played a great part in subsequent events. One was the exclusion of women from the succession by the adoption of the Salic Law. Then, in order to curb the degeneracy or to reinforce the inefficiency of the hereditary ruler, there was created the office of ***Maire du Palais,*** a modest title which contained the germ of the future, not alone of France, but of the world.

To imperfect human vision it would have seemed at the time a fatal mistake to bury out of sight the refinements which a Latin civilization had been for nearly five centuries planting in Gaul. But so often has this been repeated in the history of the world, one is compelled to recognize it as a part of the evolutionary method. Again and again have we seen old civilizations effaced by barbarians. But these barbarians with their coarseness and brutality have usually brought something better than refinement; a spirit so transforming, so vitalizing, that we are compelled to believe it was the end sought in the catastrophe we deplore: that is, a spirit of liberty, a sense of personal independence, without which the refinements of art, even reinforced by genius, are unavailing. Such was undoubtedly the invigorating leaven brought into Gaul by the Frank, although for a time he succumbed to the enervating Gallic influence, and, while conquering and subduing, was himself conquered and subdued.

The cultivated Roman in his toga appealed to the imagination of the fine barbarian; the habits of the Romanized cities were a tempting model for imitation. Bridges, aqueducts, palaces, with their splendid mingling of strength and beauty, fragments of which still linger to convince us of our inferiority, these were awe-inspiring to the Frank and filled him with longings to drink deep at this fountain of civilization. The heroic strain brought by Clovis was quickly enfeebled and debauched by luxury. The court of the Merovingian king became a miserable assemblage of half-Romanized barbarians covered with the frayed and worn-out mantle of imperialism. It is a strange picture we have of this descendant of Clovis, this Roi Fainéant (Do-nothing King) in a royal procession on a state occasion. Curled and perfumed, he emerges from the ***Palais des Thermes,*** attended in great pomp by Romans and Romanized Frankish warriors. Then, in remembrance of the primitive simplicity of his ancestral line, sitting alone in a wagon drawn by bullocks, he leads the pageant through the narrow streets of old Paris.

But while masquerading as a simple barbarian he was only a poor imitator of the vices and dregs of a perishing civilization. But in proof that virility was still a characteristic of the Frank in Gaul, we are told that while the Church and the offices of State were filled by Romans or Gallo-Romans, the army at this time was composed entirely of Franks.

With the degeneracy of these Rois Fainéants the kingdom of Clovis was gradually shrinking, and men were already waiting to seize the power as it fell from incompetent hands. When Clovis made gifts of large estates to reward, or to purchase, followers, Roman or Gallic, he laid the foundations of a system which would prove fatal to his successors. With these estates came titles and authority, multiplying and growing with each succeeding reign. A count, who was the chief officer of a county, was in fact the sovereign of a small state, and so on a smaller scale were a duke or a marquis. And it was to these smaller bodies that the power naturally gravitated as it vanished from the throne.

This meant disintegration into helpless fragments, and this meant the end of a Frankish kingdom, unless some power should arise great enough to compel the crumbling state to become homogeneous.

It was a Romanized-Frankish family dwelling in the Valley of the Rhine which saved the kingdom of Clovis from this fate. France had already fallen apart into an eastern and a western kingdom, known respectively as **Austrasia** and **Neustria.** A certain Duke of Austrasia, known as Pepin the Elder, was the forerunner of the Carlovingian line of kings. With him the centralizing force began to work with saving power. The one end kept in view was the restoration of the power of kingship—the strengthening of the power at the centre. To this end, from generation to generation, these early Pepins steadily moved. In 687 Pepin the Younger, grandson of the Elder, by a victory at Testry over Neustria, brought together these two sundered divisions under himself, with the new title Duke of the Franks. The Pepins had already succeeded in making the office of Maire du Palais hereditary in their family, and in the year A.D. 732, Charles, son and successor of Pepin the Younger, made himself forever the hero not of France alone, but of Christendom, by driving the Saracen invasion back over the Pyrenees, and was in turn succeeded by his son, Pepin the Short, who seized the Merovingian crown itself; this remarkable family, the appointed channel for the centralizing forces, reaching its climax in his son Charlemagne, creator of a Holy Roman Empire.

There had appeared an enemy to the true faith more to be feared than paganism.

Less than one hundred years after the death of Clovis, there had come out of Asia, that birthplace of religions, a new faith, which was destined to be for centuries the scourge of Christendom, and which to-day rules one-third of the human family.

Zoroaster, Buddha, Christ, had successively come with saving message to humanity, and now (A.D. 600) Mahomet believed himself divinely appointed to drive out of Arabia the idolatry of ancient Magianism (the religion of Zoroaster).

Christianity had passed through strange vicissitudes. Kings, emperors, popes, and bishops had been terrible custodians of its truths; and while many still held it in its primitive purity, ecclesiastics were fiercely fighting over the nature of the Trinity, the divinity of the Virgin Mother, and the Church was shaken to its foundation by furious factions.

In this hour of weakness the Persians (A.D. 590) had conquered Asia Minor. Bethlehem, Gethsemane, and Calvary were profaned; the Holy Sepulchre had been burned, and the cross carried off amid shouts of laughter. Magianism had insulted Christianity, and no miracle had interposed! The heavens did not roll asunder, nor did the earth open her abysses to swallow them up. There was consternation and doubt in Christendom.

Such was the state of the Church when Mahometanism came into existence. "There is but one God, and Mahomet is his Prophet" Such was its battle-cry and its creed, and the moral precepts of the Koran were its gospel. There seems nothing in this to account for the mad enthusiasm and the passion for worship in its followers. But in less than a hundred years this lion out of Arabia had subjugated Syria, Mesopotamia, Egypt, Northern Africa, and the Spanish Peninsula. Now, sword in one hand and the Koran in the other, the Mahometan had crossed the Pyrenees and was in Southern Gaul.

Under the strange magic of this faith the largest religious empire the world had known had sprung into existence, stretching from the Chinese Wall to the Atlantic; from the Caspian to the Indian Ocean; and Jerusalem, the metropolis of Christianity—Jerusalem, the Mecca of the Christian—was lost! The Crescent floated over the birthplace of our Lord, and, notwithstanding the temporary successes of the Crusades, it does to this day.

If the Pyrenees were passed the very existence of Christendom was threatened. Charles Martel, the grandfather of Charlemagne, averted this danger when he stayed the infidel flood at the battle of Tours, A.D. 732.

The Merovingian kings, if not devout, were faithful sons of the Church, and when the pope appealed to the last Merovingian king to protect him from the Lombards, near the end of the eighth century, Pepin, then Maire du Palais, but holding supreme power, twice crossed the Alps with an army, wrested five cities and a large extent of territory from the enemies of the pope, which, upon parting, he tossed as a gift into the lap of the Church. And this, known as the ***Donation of Pepin,*** was the beginning of the temporal power of the popes in Italy. So when Pepin resolved to assume the crown, Pope Zacharias in gratitude sanctioned the audacious act, by sending his representative to place the symbol of power upon the head of this faithful son and usurper! (A.D. 751.)

But this was only the stepping-stone for a greater elevation. When Pope Adrian I. again needed protection from the Lombard, a greater than Pepin was wearing the crown his father had audaciously snatched.

CHAPTER V.

AGAINST the dark background of European history, and with the broad level of obscurity stretching over the ages at its feet, there rises one shining pinnacle. Considered as man or sovereign, Charlemagne is one of the most impressive figures in history. His seven feet of stature clad in shining steel, his masterful grasp of the forces of his time, his splendid intelligence, instinct even then with the modern spirit, all combine to elevate him in solitary grandeur.

Charlemagne found France in disorder measureless, and apparently insurmountable. Barbarian invasion without, and anarchy within; Saxon paganism pressing in upon the north, and Asiatic Islamism upon the south and west; a host of forces struggling for dominion in a nation brutish, ignorant, and without cohesion.

It is the attribute of genius to discern opportunity where others see nothing. Charlemagne saw rising out of this chaos a great resuscitated Roman Empire, which should be at the same time a spiritual and Christian empire as well. Saxons, Slavs, Huns, Lombards, Arabs, came under his compelling grasp; these antagonistic races all held together by the force of one terrible will, in unnatural combination with France. No political liberties, no popular assemblies discussing public measures; it is Charlemagne alone who fills the picture; it is absolutism—marked by prudence, ability, and grandeur, but still, absolutism.

The pope looked approvingly upon this son of the Church, by whose order 4,500 pagan heads could be cut off in one day, and a whole army compelled to baptism in an afternoon. Here was a champion to be propitiated. Charlemagne, on the other hand, saw in the Church the most compliant and effective means to empire.

His fertile mind was conceiving a vast design by which he might reign over a resuscitated Roman Empire. In the dual sovereignty of his dream, the pope was to be the spiritual and he the temporal head. Mutually dependent upon each other, the election of the pope would not be valid without his consent. Nor would the emperor be emperor until crowned by the pope The Church might use him as a sword, but he would wear the Church as a precious jewel in his crown.

It was a splendid dream, splendidly realized; the most imposing of human successes, and the most impressive of human failures. It seems designed as a lesson for the human race in the transitory nature of power applied from without.

A pyramid of such colossal proportions could only be kept from falling in pieces by another Colossus like himself. The vast fabric resting upon one human will, passed with its creator; was gone like a shadow when he was gone.

It will be remembered that the Roman Empire in its decay fell into two parts, a Western and an Eastern empire. The dying embers of the Western empire, which had been fanned into a feeble flame in the sixth century by Justinian, Emperor of the East, were threatened with complete extinguishment by the Lombards in the eighth; from which calamity they were saved, as we have seen, by Pepin. So when the Franks were again appealed to, Charlemagne saw his opportunity. With plans fully matured he responded, and with the consent and acquiescence of the pope he took formal possession of the whole of Italy, annexing to his own dominions the crumbling wreck of a magnificent past. And when Leo III. placed upon his head the crown, and pronounced "Carolus-Magnus, by the grace of God Emperor of the Holy Roman Empire" (A.D. 800), the authority of the pope was placed upon unassailable heights, and France had become the centre of a world-wide dominion.

Little did pope or emperor dream of what was to happen; that after a brief and dazzling interlude the imperial crown would never be worn in France; and that the popes would for centuries be insulted and treated as contumacious vassals by German emperors. And France—France, the centre of this dream of a magnificent unity—in less than fifty years, with her native incohesiveness, and in the irony of fate, would have broken into fifty-nine fragments, loosely held together by a feeble Carlovingian king.

The plan of a dual sovereignty of pope and emperor might have been wise had both been immortal! But it was the triple division of the empire brought about by Charlemagne's three grandsons which overthrew the entire scheme of its founder.

Upon the death of Charlemagne, in A.D. 814, the crown and the sceptre of the empire passed to his son Louis (the later form of Clovis). This feeble son of Charlemagne, known as Louis the Débonnaire, struggled under the weight of the crumbling mass until his death in 840. Then Charlemagne's three ambitious grandsons fought for the great inheritance. Lothaire, who claimed the whole by right of primogeniture, was defeated at the battle of Fontenay in Burgundy, and by the treaty of Verdun in 843 the partition of the empire was consummated; the title of emperor passing to Lothaire, the eldest, along with Italy and a strip of territory extending to the North Sea, all west of that being arbitrarily called France, and all east of it Germany.

So the European drama was unfolding upon lines entirely unexpected. Not only had the empire fallen apart into three grand divisions, but France itself was disintegrating, was in fact a mass of rival states, with counts, princes, marquises, and a score of other petty potentates struggling for supremacy.

The rough outlines of something greater than France—the outlines of a future Europe—were being drawn. It is easy to see now what was then so incomprehensible: that from the chaos of barbarism left by the Teuton flood, there were emerging in that ninth century a group of states with definite outlines, and the larger organism of Europe was coming into form. The treaty of Verdun (843) had roughly separated *Italy, France,* and *Germany.* At the same time the Heptarchy in Britain had been consolidated into *England* under King Alfred; while an obscure Scandinavian adventurer named Rurik, quite unobserved, was bringing into political unity, and reigning at Kieff as Grand Duke over what was to become *Russia. Spain,* quite apart from all this movement, had entered upon those seven centuries of struggle with Saracen and Moor, that struggle of unmatched devotion and tenacity of purpose which is really the great epic of history.

Those ambitious and too powerful vassals were not the greatest evils menacing the Carlovingian kings. It was the incessant invasions of a race of barbarians coming out of the north, which was going to bury the past under a ruin of a different sort. There seemed no defence from these Northmen, as they were called, who swarmed like destroying insects upon the coast, up the rivers, and over the lands; three times sacked Paris, the scars to-day being visible in that impressive Roman ruin, the ***Palais des Thermes,*** the home of the Cæsars, and of the Merovingian kings, which they partially burned.

Fortified castles with towers and moats and drawbridges sprang up all over the kingdom for the protection of the rich. After seven invasions all the old cities, Rouen, Nantes, Bordeaux, Toulouse, Orleans, Beauvais, had been devastated, and France in coat of mail was hiding behind stone walls.

In looking through the vista of centuries it is easy to read the eternal purpose in the chain of cause and effect; and also to see that events, no less than kings, have their pedigrees. The terrible child of the Northman was the ***Feudal System;*** which was again the father of those romantic and picturesque children, the ***Crusades;*** and these, the creators of a European civilization, whose children we are!

Who can imagine the course of history with any one of these removed—each an apparently inevitable step in the unfolding of a mighty design, utterly incomprehensible at the time?

CHAPTER VI.

SOMEONE has said that "the Lord must like common people, because he made so many of them." The path for the common people in France at this time led through heavy shadows. But a darker time was approaching. A system of oppression was maturing which was soon to envelop them in the obscurity of darkest night.

Those Scandinavian freebooters called Northmen, and later Normans, were the scourge of the kingdom. Nothing was safe from their insolent courage and rapacity.

The rich could intrench themselves in stone fortresses, with moats and drawbridges, and be in comparative security, but the poor were utterly defenceless against this perennial destroyer. The result was a compact between the powerful and the weak, which was the beginning of the feudal system. It was in effect an exchange of protection for service and fealty. You give us absolute control of your persons—your military service when required, and a portion of your substance and the fruit of your toil—and we will in exchange give you our fortified castles as a refuge from the Northmen. Such was the offer. It was a choice between vassalage, serfdom, or destruction outright.

Simple enough in its beginnings, this became a ramified system of oppression, a curious network of authority, ingeniously controlling an entire people. The conditions upon which was engrafted this compact were of great antiquity, had indeed been brought across the Rhine by the German conquerors; but the Northmen were the impelling cause of the swift development of feudalism in France.

Charlemagne had felt grave apprehensions of evil from these robber incursions, but could not have conceived of a result such as this, the most oppressive system ever fastened upon a nation, and one which would at the same time sap the foundations of royalty itself.

The theory was that the king was absolute owner of all the territory; the great lords holding their titles from him on condition of military service, their vassals pledging military service and obedience to them again on similar terms, and sub-vassals again to them repeating the pledge; and so on in descending chain, until at last the serf, that wretched being whom none looks up to nor fears, is ground to powder beneath the superimposed mass; no appeal from the authority, no escape from the caprice or cruelty of his feudal lord. Could any scales weigh, could any words measure the suffering which must have been endured? Is it strange that, with every aspiration thwarted, hope stifled, Europe sank into the long sleep of the Middle Ages?

It is easy to conceive that, under such a system, where all the affairs of the realm were adjusted by individual rulers with unlimited power, and where the great barons could make war upon each other without authorization from the king, by the time this nominal head of the entire system was reached there remained nothing for him to do. In fact, there was not left one vestige of kingly authority, and Carlovingian rulers were almost as insignificant as their Merovingian predecessors. France had, instead of one great sovereign, one hundred and fifty petty ones!

In A.D. 911 the Northmen were offered the province henceforth known as Normandy, upon condition of their acceptance of the religion and submission to the laws of the realm. Rollo, the disreputable robber-chief, took the oath of fealty to the King of France, his suzerain, and Christian baptism transformed him into respectable, law-abiding Robert, Duke of Normandy.

So, the enemy had become a vassal. The pirate of the North Sea had taken his place among the Christian chivalry of Europe, as one of the twelve peers of France. It was less than a century since the death of Charlemagne, and the office of king had grown almost as helpless as in the period of the Rois Fainéants. Under the stress of the continuous invasions, by perfectly natural process the central authority had passed to the feudal magnates. Many of the feudal states had actually organized into independent governing bodies. The struggle with the Northmen ended, France, dismembered, exhausted, was lying prostrate. A king stripped of every kingly attribute at one extreme of the social system, and a people trampled into the very dust by feudal oppression at the other. Owners of nothing, not even of themselves, they might not fish in the streams, nor hunt in the forests, unless the privilege was bestowed; and with their lives spent in fighting the incessant private wars of their lords, there seemed no room for them in the world, nor for hope in their hearts. With the king effaced, and the people effaced, there remained only bands of feudal barons trying to efface each other!

As in the last days of the Merovingians, light came from an unexpected quarter. The tide turned toward centralization. Robert the Strong, a man of obscure family, who had laid down his life in a very heroic resistance to the Northmen, had won the titles "Count of Paris" and "Duke of France," which he bequeathed, with the estates attached to them, to his successors.

Somewhat after the manner of the Pepins, this powerful and resourceful family by sheer native ability grasped one after another the sources of power in the state; and in the year 987 the dynasty established by Pepin disappeared, and Hugh Capet, Count of Paris and Abbot, was declared by the Pope of Rome to be "King of France, in virtue of his great deeds." It was the ecclesiastical office of this descendant of Robert the Strong which gave the name to the dynasty that had come to save France a second time from disintegration. Because he was the wearer of the ***Chapet,*** or ***Cope,*** the name ***Chapet,*** or ***Capet,*** became that of the line.

There now commenced a struggle between the antagonistic principles of royalty and aristocracy; a conflict which was going to last nearly five centuries, covering that dreary twilight known as the Dark Ages—a time when, had it not been for the Christian Church and for the torch of the Saracen in Spain, the light of civilization would really have been extinguished, and the slender thread of connection with a great past have been broken.

In the helpless misery existing in France at this time, the Church saw its opportunity. To that silent, humble, forgotten multitude without life or hope in the world, she offered refuge, peace, consolation, and thus forever bound to her the poor of Christendom; by this means establishing in the end an ecclesiastical dominion to which kings and peerage would be compelled to bow.

If one would know how kings submitted to the authority of the Church at this time, let him read the story of the good King Robert, second in the Capetian line, who for marrying the gentle Bertha, his cousin fourth removed, suffered the punishment of excommunication; was treated as a moral leper in his own palace; cut off from contact with human kind and from sound of human voice; the dishes from which he ate, the clothes he wore, destroyed, until repentant and heart-broken they consented to part and to break the bond of their union forever.

It was the despair in the heart of the nation which gave intensity to the religious instinct at this time. And when pestilence came, and neither rich nor poor could escape, conscience-stricken barons also trembled. A belief began to prevail that the end of the world was at hand. Did not the Book, of Revelation say that one thousand years from the birth of Christ the great dragon was to be let loose and the earth was to be destroyed?

As the hour of doom approached, labor ceased, the fields were untouched, and when to pestilence and despair was added famine, then men's hearts failed them even under coats of mail. The Church came to the rescue with the "Truce of God," which, in the hope of appeasing an avenging God, forbade private wars during certain periods in the ecclesiastical year. Repentant barons, with a similar hope, made peace with their neighbors, and their swords rusted as they built monasteries and chapels; or some not yet obtaining peace, and perhaps restless with their occupation gone, made pilgrimages to Rome, to pray at the graves of Peter and Paul, and still others even to Jerusalem, that the breath from Calvary might whiten their sin-steeped souls.

It is interesting to note that among these penitent pilgrims, sixty years before the first Crusade, was that Duke of Normandy known as "Robert the Devil," whose pagan ancestor only a century before had been the terror of European civilization, and whose son, thirty years later, was to wear the crown of England.

In this way were the currents setting steadily toward the Holy Sepulchre as the panacea for human woes which were sent by an avenging God. These were the first stirrings of the breath of the coming storm which in eight successive waves was soon to sweep over Europe. The way was preparing for the great event of the Middle Ages.

Whatever its motives, the abstaining from slaughter, and the building of cathedrals and monasteries and abbeys, was weaving a mantle of beauty for France, which she still proudly wears. And the greatest of the builders was the Duke of Normandy; and it is to his dukedom the art student turns for the most perfect blending of grace and grandeur, characteristic of the early style. The marvel to which this is intended to draw attention is the preeminent position swiftly attained in France by this brilliant race, in every department of living. It would seem that France did not adopt this terrible child from the north, but that he adopted France, and changed and gave color to her whole future. It was a tempestuous element, but it was new life, and it is impossible to conceive of what that country would have been without this stimulating, brilliant infusion into its national life.

With such marvellous facility did this people adopt the speech and manners of their neighbors, that in the year 1066 they were prepared to instruct the Britons in the ways of a more polished civilization. Only a century before the birth of William the Conqueror, his ancestors had lived by looting. They were highwaymen and robbers by profession. His mother, a Norman peasant girl, daughter of a tanner, won the love of that gay duke known as "Robert the Devil." William, the child of this unconsecrated union, upon the death of his father succeeded to the dukedom. One of the steps in the rapid climb of this family of Rollo had been a marriage connecting them with the royal family of England. King Edward, William's remote cousin, died without an heir. Here was an opportunity. With sixty thousand Norman adventurers like himself, William started with the desperate purpose of invading England and wresting the crown from his cousin Harold.

It was not the first time the Northman had invaded England. But never before had he come bringing a higher civilization, and under the banner of the Church! In a few weeks Harold, last king of the Saxons, was dead, and William, Duke of Normandy, was William I, King of England.

Philip, King of France, saw with dismay his richest province ruled by a king of England, and his own vassal wearing a crown with power superior to his own! A door had thus opened through which would enter entangling complications and countless woes in the future.

While William was trampling England into the dust, and with pitiless hand rivetting a feudal chain upon the Saxons, another and greater centre of power was developing at Rome, where the monk Hildebrand, who had now become Pope Gregory VII., claimed a universal sovereignty from which there was no appeal. Christ was King of Kings. So, as His vicegerent upon earth, the authority of the pope was absolute in Christendom.

The moment of this supreme elevation in the Church was reached at Canossa, 1072, when Henry, the excommunicated Emperor of Germany, came barefooted, in winter, and prostrated himself before Gregory VII. If Charlemagne had worn the Church as a precious jewel in his crown in the ninth century, now in the eleventh the Church wore all the European states as a tiara of jewels in her mitre. With supreme wisdom, and with a sure instinct for power, her supremacy had been rooted first in the hearts of the people, then the mailed hand laid upon their rulers.

CHAPTER VII.

THE corner-stone of the social structure in France was the dogma that work was degrading; and not only manual labor, but anything done with the object of producing wealth was a degradation. The only honorable occupation for a gentleman was either to pray or to fight

Society in France was, therefore, divided into three classes: the *Clergy,* called the "First Estate"; the *Nobility,* composing the "Second Estate," and the working and trading classes, the "Third Estate," or Tiers État.

Out of reverence for their spiritual office, precedence in rank was given to the clergy. But the actual ruling class was the nobility, The business of the clergy was to minister to souls. The business of the nobility was warfare. That of the third estate, the toiling class, being to **support the other two.** And whatever existed in the form of property or wealth in feudal times was produced by the Tiers État.

The lowest stratum of the third estate was composed of "serfs." A serf belonged absolutely, with all that he possessed, to his lord. He was attached to his land, as are the trees which are rooted in it. There was, however, a class of serfs above this whom we should now call slaves, but who were by French law then designated as *Freemen.*

A freeman might go and come under certain restrictions. But this did not by any means imply that he was freed from the proprietor to whom he belonged, to whom he was inevitably bound for military service, or for such contributions or claims as might be levied upon him.

As was to be expected, it was in the cities that this half-emancipated class congregated; these cities as naturally becoming the centres of the various industries required to supply the necessities and luxuries of the two ruling classes. In this way there were being created various centres of wealth, which meant power, and which would have to be reckoned with in the future.

The thin edge of the wedge was inserted when individual freemen offered money to their hard-pressed feudal lords in exchange for certain privileges, and then for charters. And as more money was needed by proprietors for their lavish expenditures, more freedom and more charters were acquired, until, having purchased immunities and privileges enough to make them to some extent self-governing, the town became what was called a *commune.*

It was Louis VI., fifth king in the Capetian line, who completed this work of emancipation by recognizing the communes as free cities, and bestowing franchises clearly defining their rights. By this act the body of the manufacturing class, or *burgesses,* was recognized as part of the body politic, and was *enfranchised.*

A free city was a small republic. The entire body of inhabitants must take the communal oath, and when summoned by the tolling of the bell must all appear at the meeting of the General Assembly for the purpose of choosing their magistrates. This done, the assembly dissolved, and the magistrates were left with a free hand to rule or ruin, until checked by popular outbreak or a new election.

As is always the case, time developed two classes: an inferior population, with a furious spirit of democracy, and a superior class, more conservative, and desirous of keeping peace with the great proprietors.

In this simple, humble fashion were the people groping toward freedom, and experimenting with the alphabet of self-government.

The acknowledgment of the free cities by Louis VI., was the first move toward an alliance between the king and the people; an alliance which would eventually wrest the power from the hands of the nobles. But that end was still far off. Another accession to the kingly power came in the succeeding reign when Louis VII. married Eleanor, daughter of the Duke of Aquitaine; and her great inheritance, the largest of the feudal states, was thereby annexed to the crown: a marriage which made some troublesome chapters in the history of two kingdoms, of which we shall hear later. But, in the duel between king and peerage, the balance of power was moving toward the throne.

At the time these things were happening that great event, the Crusades, had already commenced.

It was in 1095 that Peter the Hermit, returning from a pilgrimage, by command of the Pope went throughout Europe proclaiming the desecration of the holy places. At a council held at Clermont in France, 1095, the first Crusade was proclaimed by Urban II. Led by Peter the Hermit, a vast undisciplined host, without preparation, rushed indiscriminately toward Asia Minor, perishing by famine, disease, and the sword before they reached their goal. Undismayed by this, another Crusade was immediately organized under the direction of the greatest nobles in France; and in three years (1099) the Holy City had been captured, the Cross floated over the Holy Sepulchre, and Godfrey of Boulogne, leader of the expedition, was proclaimed King of Jerusalem.

France had inaugurated the most extraordinary movement in the history of civilization. Appealing as it did to the knightly and to the romantic ideal, what an opportunity was here for idle adventurous nobles, their occupation gone through changed conditions! If the Church, by "the Truce of God," had bid them sheathe their swords, now she bade them to be drawn in the defence of all that was sacred. The entire body of nobility would have rushed if it could to the Holy Land. Poor barons sold or mortgaged their lands and their castles, and the Third Estate grew rich, and the free cities still freer, upon the necessities of the hour. But all classes, from king to serf, were for the first time moved by a common sentiment; and not alone France, but the choicest and best of Europe was poured in one great volume of passionate zeal into those successive waves which eight times inundated Palestine. Private interests sacrificed or forgotten, life, treasure, all eagerly given, for what? That a small bit of territory a thousand miles distant be torn from profaning infidels, because it was the birthplace of a religion these champions failed to comprehend; a religion worn upon their battle-flags but not in their hearts.

The second Crusade, 1147, was led by Conrad, Emperor of Germany, and Louis VII. of France. The profligate conduct of Queen Eleanor, who accompanied her royal consort, led to serious political conditions. Louis appealed to the pope, who consented to the divorce he desired. This proved simply an exchange of thrones for the fascinating Eleanor. Henry II. of England, already the possessor of immense estates in France, inherited from his father, realized that with Aquitaine, Queen Eleanor's dowry, added to his own, and these again to Normandy, a marriage with the divorced wife of his rival would make him possessor of more than three times the size of the domain controlled by the French king.

The marriage was solemnized in 1152, and France saw her war with the feudal barons overshadowed by the fight for her very life with England, who had fastened this tremendous grasp upon her kingdom.

The first truly great Capetian king came with this emergency. Philip Augustus, son of Louis VII, in the year 1180, when only fifteen years of age, seized the reins with the hand of a born ruler. Before he was twenty-one he had broken up a combination of feudal barons against him. Then he turned to England. Queen Eleanor and her sons were conspiring against Henry II. So he made friends with them. The palace on the island in the Seine was an asylum where John and Richard might plot against their father. And when a third Crusade was planned, 1189, it; had as leaders Philip Augustus of France, Richard I, who had just succeeded his father, Henry II., as King of England, and Barbarossa (Frederick. I.), the great Emperor of Germany. Before the Holy Land was reached the wise and crafty Philip Augustus and the fiery Richard had quarrelled.

Philip had been carefully observing these two brothers who were successively to wear the crown of England. He knew the foibles of the romantic and picturesque Richard; and he also knew that John, corrupt to the core, was a traitor to whom no trust would be sacred. In his own cold-blooded fashion he intended to use them both.

John had conspired against his own father, now Philip would help him to supplant his brother, while Richard was safely occupied in Palestine. And when he had made John king, he, Philip Augustus, was to be rewarded by the gift of Normandy! With this in view, Philip returned to France. It was an ingenious plot, but all was spoiled by Richard's safe return from the thrilling adventures of the Crusade. In 1199, however, the crown passed naturally to John by the death of his brother, and this vicious son of Eleanor was King of England.

There were other means of recovering his lost possessions. Philip espoused the cause of the young Arthur, John's nephew, a rival claimant to the English throne. And when that ill-fated Prince was murdered, as is believed by the orders of his uncle, for this and other offences King John, as Duke of Normandy—thence vassal to the King of France—was summoned to be tried by his peers.

When after oft-repeated summons John refused to appear at Philip's court, by feudal law the King of France had legal authority to take possession of the dukedom.

In vain did King John strive to defend by arms his vanishing possessions. In the war which ensued, all north of the Loire was seized by Philip, and at one stroke he had mastered his enemies at home and abroad.

Not only were Normandy, Anjou, Touraine, and Poitou restored to France, but they were hereafter to be held, not by dukes and counts, as before, but by the king, as a part of the royal domain. And kingship, towering high above all the great barons of France, had for the first time become a reality.

It was Philip's policy of expansion which gave color to his reign; not an expansion which would bring extension into foreign lands, but solidity and firmness of outline to France itself. We have seen how and why this policy was vigorously carried out in the north. The growth toward the south is a less pleasant story.

The province of Toulouse, nominally subject to France, was actually ruled by Raymond VI., "by grace of God" Count of Toulouse. Perhaps if this province had not possessed and controlled several ports on the Mediterranean, while France had none at all, it might not have been discovered that this home of the "gay science," and of minstrelsy, and of all that was gentle and refining, was in fact the nursery of a dangerous heresy, and that the poetic, music-loving children of Provence reviled the cross and worshipped the devil!

We can easily imagine that in this highly developed community there had arisen a spirit of inquiry into prevailing conditions and beliefs in the Church. And we can also imagine that a crafty sovereign saw in this an opportunity to serve his own ends. And so, Pope Innocent III. ordered a Crusade, and John de Mont-fort not only opened up the Mediterranean ports for Philip, but brought Toulouse, the greatest of the remaining feudal states, into subjection to the King of France; at the same time forever silencing the voice of the heretic, of the minstrel, and of the harp; even the speech, with its delicate inflections and musical intonations, disappeared, to be heard nevermore. Such, in brief, is the story of the "Albigensian War," so called on account of the heresy having been brought into Provence by the Albigenses from Switzerland.

After a century and a half Normandy was restored. Its reabsorption into France marked the parting of the ways in two kingdoms. ***Kingship*** was reinforced in one, and ***citizenship*** developed in the other. In England the nobles and the people drew closer together, resolved to defend themselves from a vicious king, and this determined effort to curtail the royal prerogative produced the ***Magna Charta,*** which forever secured the liberties of Englishmen (1215). In France, on the contrary, the power was moved in one volume toward the king and despotism. Both nations were in the hands of fate—a fate, too, which was using unscrupulous men to accomplish its great purposes for each.

But however we may disparage Philip's heart and aims, no one can deny the breadth and superiority of his mind and his statesmanship. He was a Charlemagne made on a smaller scale, and without a conscience. Not one of the successors of Clovis or of Pepin had so intelligently grasped the sources of permanent growth in a nation. He may have been false of tongue and unprincipled in deed, but he took the free cities under his personal protection, opened up trade with foreign lands, beautified Paris and France. He may, under the cloak of religion, have permitted unjustifiable cruelties against the most innocent, the most gifted province in Europe, in order to secure access to the sea for France. But he left the ***communes*** richer and happier, his kingdom freer from local tyrannies, transformed from a pandemonium of struggling knights and barons into the nearest approach yet realized to a modern state.

CHAPTER VIII.

IF the Crusades had strengthened the power of the Church, they had at the same time brought about an expansion of thought which was undermining it Men were beginning to think, to inquire, and then to doubt. How could sensuality and vice at Rome be reconciled with a divine infallibility? If the ballad-poetry of Provence satirized the lives and manners of the priests, was it not dealing with what was true?

During the reign of Philip's father, a pale, studious youth was pacing the cloisters on the banks of the Seine, by the side of Notre Dame. He was thinking upon these things. And "as he mused the fire burned." This was Abelard. The intellectual awakening brought about by the lectures of this most learned and accomplished man of his time produced an epoch. He spoke to his disciples in the open air, as no building could hold the thousands who hung upon his lips. This movement became localized; a faubourg of students was created with their multiform activities. It became a quarter by itself—a noisy, turbulent, agitated quarter—where the only luxury enjoyed was an expanding thought, and where Latin was the spoken language. And so it happened that the *Quarter Latin* came into existence.

But while the place remains, the man quickly passed off the scene. He was silenced, his teachings condemned by a Church council at Soissons, and he immured for life in the Monastery of Cluny, to be treasured in the heart of humanity as a martyr to truth, and as the lover of Eloise, in that sad romance of the twelfth century.

After a brief reign of three years Louis VIII., son and successor of Philip, was dead, and Louis IX., under the regency of his mother, "Blanche of Castile," was proclaimed king. The same family, which later gave Isabella to Spain, also bestowed upon France this wise, intrepid woman at a critical time.

With a boy of eleven and a woman of thirty-eight years upon the throne, the time seemed propitious for the barons to recover the power Philip had wrung from them, and to reduce kingship to its former humble position.

With this purpose a powerful coalition was formed, embracing the barons north and south, chief among whom was Raymond of Toulouse. By force of arms, and by diplomacy, Blanche of Castile met this crisis with astonishing courage and address. The free cities sprang to her assistance; and not only was the coalition broken, but there was formed a bond between the crown and the people, leaving the throne stronger than before.

Blanche showed great political wisdom in arranging for the marriage of her son with the daughter of the Count of Provence; thus capturing and securing the loyalty of this most powerful and disaffected state, which was making common cause with Toulouse against the king. And it is with mingled pity and rejoicing that we hear of Raymond VII. of Toulouse, once champion of the Albigenses—warrior, poet, troubadour, and heretic—scourge in hand and barefooted, at the porch of Notre Dame, doing penance for his sins against the Church.

With Louis IX. on the throne a new day had dawned for France. Louis was not a great soldier. His reign was not one of territorial expansion but of wise administration, giving permanence and solidity to what already existed. We are apt to think of Philip's heavenly minded grandson chiefly as a saint. But his service to the state was enduring and of the first magnitude, because it dealt with the sources of things. When he established a King's Court, which was a court of appeal from the rude justice, or injustice, of feudal counts, he undermined the foundation of feudal power. In bestowing the *right of appeal,* his protecting hand reached down to the poorest man in the realm. And when bewildered barons heard the uncomprehended language of the law-courts, and heard men not of their own order declaring private wars punishable by death, they felt their power slipping from under them, and that they were coming into a new sort of world.

One of the greatest acts of this reign was the abolishing of the double allegiance, which had wrought such trouble since the Duke of Normandy's conquest of England. Feudal proprietors were forbidden to hold territory under a foreign king; and henceforth no conquered province could acknowledge allegiance to an English king; nor would an English king again be vassal to a king of France.

But in so fortifying his throne, this best of kings, and of men, would have been surprised had he been told that he was preparing the way for the greatest tragedy in history; that he was creating an absolute despotism which five hundred years later would require a revolution of unprecedented horror for its removal. Such was the fact. Every wise act in this reign was prompted by the spirit of fairness and justice. And if at the same time these acts were drawing all the forces in the state to a central point, under the control of a single hand, it was the best development for France under existing conditions.

Saint though he was, and almost fanatic in his devotion to the Church, Louis resisted the pope or the bishop, if unjust, with as much energy as one of his own barons; and, in the same spirit of fairness, would punish his own too zealous defenders who had infringed upon the feudal rights of the peerage.

This was Louis the king. But it is Louis the saint who holds the eye on the world's canvas. The real life was to him the life of the soul. Francis Assisi himself did not live in an atmosphere of greater spiritual exaltation than this devout and heavenly grandson of Philip Augustus! No monk in the Dark Ages attached such sanctity to relics. "When a portion of the crown of thorns was sent to him from Jerusalem, he built that exquisite **Sainte Chapelle** for its reception; and barefooted, bareheaded, carried it himself in solemn procession from Vincennes to Paris, placing it with reverent hands in that shrine we may visit to-day.

Christian knighthood had reached its one perfect flower in Louis; and the Crusades fittingly closed with the life of the most saintly crusader. His first Crusade was disastrous, occupying years of his life; his mother, Blanche of Castile, dying during his absence. His second and last was more costly still. Near the ruins of Carthage, where he was in conflict with a Mohometan band, he was stricken with fever and died (1270).

Louis's brother, Charles of Anjou, is said to have led him into this fatal attempt, for his own purposes. Charles, of very different memory, was at this time, by invitation of the pope, occupying the double throne of Naples and Sicily. And he it was who provoked by his cruelties that frightful outbreak known as the "Sicilian Vespers," in 1283.

The Crusades had lasted from 1095 to 1270. The purpose for which they were undertaken had signally failed. Jerusalem, captured in the first Crusade, was lost in the second, and never recovered. And so ineffectual had been the expenditure of life, fortune, and enthusiasm that the last Crusade was not even fought in Palestine, but on the shores of North Africa.

But something had been accomplished which none had foreseen: a result of greater magnitude than territorial possession of the Holy Land. Through the broadening of men's views, and the common heritage of a great experience, a group of isolated kingdoms had been drawn into fraternal relations, and a European civilization had commenced.

There had been many surprises. Close contact had softened prejudices. The infidel had found that the crusader was something more than the most brutal and stupid of barbarians, as he had supposed; and the crusader, that the profaning infidel was not the monster he expected to find. In fact, the European discovered that in the Saracen and the Greek they met a civilization much more advanced, more learned, and more polished than their own. More civilization was brought out of the East than was carried into it by its Christian invaders. And it was through this strange and disastrous experience that the art and the thought of Europe received its first impulse toward a great future.

During the fifteen years of the reign of Louis's son, Philip III., France moved on under the momentum received from his father. But the succeeding reign of Philip IV. was epoch-making. That imperious, strong-willed son of Saint Louis demanded that the clergy should share the state's burden by contributing to its revenue. Pope Boniface VIII, imperious and strong-willed as he, immediately issued a bull, forbidding the clergy to pay, or the officers to receive, such taxes. The answer to this was a royal edict forbidding the exportation of precious metals (of course including money) from France to Italy, thus cutting off from the pope the large revenue from the Church in France.

The quarrel resolved itself at last into a question of the relative authority of king and pope in the kingdom. In order to fortify his position, and perhaps to show his contempt for clergy and barons alike, Philip took a step which profoundly affected the future of France. At a great council summoned to consider these papal claims, he commanded the presence not only of the ecclesiastics and nobles, the two governing estates, but also summoned the representatives of the towns and cities—the Tiers État! Prelate, baron, and bourgeois for the first time met in a Council of State.

A king who was the impersonation of absolutism had created the ***States-General*** (1302); had forged the instrument which would eventually effect for France a deliverance from monarchy itself!

The cause of the king was sustained by the council; the claims of the pope were rejected Still not satisfied, Philip then audaciously proposed a general ecclesiastical council to determine whether Boniface legitimately wore the triple crown. When the old man died, as is said from the shock of this attempt, the king was master of the situation. Gifts had already been distributed among corrupt cardinals in the conclave. The papacy was at his feet, and might be in his hand. The most dissolute of his own archbishops was selected as his tool, and, as Clement V., succeeded to the chair of St. Peter. The centre of the ecclesiastical world was then removed from Rome to Avignon, where it could be under Philip's immediate direction, and the astonishing period in the history of the papacy, known as the ***Babylonian Captivity,*** which was to last for seventy years, under seven popes, had commenced.

The Knights Templar, those appointed guardians of the Holy Sepulchre and defenders of Jerusalem, it is to be supposed were not in sympathy with these things. Whatever the cause, their extermination was decreed. Accused of impossible crimes, the whole brotherhood was arrested in one day, and, at a summary trial, condemned, Philip himself, in that old palace on the island in the Seine, giving orders for the fagots to be laid, and the immediate execution of the grand master and many others.

Philip's death, occurring as it did soon after this sacrilege, was popularly believed to be a manifestation of God's wrath; and the death of his three sons, Louis, Philip, and Charles, who successively reigned during a period of only fourteen years, leaving the family extinct, seemed a further proof that a curse rested upon the house.

The question of the succession, for the first time since Hugh Capet, was in doubt By the existing Salic Law only male descendants were eligible to the throne of France. The three sons of Philip IV. had died, leaving each a daughter, so the son of Charles of Valois, only brother of Philip IV., was the nearest in descent from Hugh Capet; and thus the crown passed to the ***Valois*** branch of the family in the person of Philip VI. (1328).

CHAPTER IX.

IN this break in the line of succession, England saw an opportunity. The mother of Edward III., King of England, was Isabella, daughter of Philip IV. Edward claimed that he, as grandson of the French king, had a claim superior to that of the nephew. A strict interpretation of the Salic Law certainly vitiated his claim of heirship through the female line. But Edward did not stand upon such a trifle as that. The stake was great, and so was the opportunity. Now England might not alone recover her lost possessions in France, but might establish a legitimate claim to the whole.

So it was that an English army was once more upon French soil, and in 1346 Edward, with his toy cannon, had won the battle of Crécy, followed by the siege and capture of Calais, which for two hundred years was to remain an English port—a thorn in the side of France.

A part of the old kingdom of Burgundy, which was called Dauphiny, dropped into the lap of Philip, this first Valois king, during his reign. The old duke, being without an heir, offered to sell this bit of territory to the King of France upon the condition that it should be kept as the personal possession of the eldest sons of the kings of France. Thenceforth the title of ***Dauphin*** was worn by the heir to the throne, until it became extinct with the son of Louis XVI. And when the feeble Philip VI. died in 1350, his son John, the first dauphin, assumed the crown of France.

John, this second Valois king, was an anachronism. A man intended for the eleventh century had been set down in the fourteenth. The restoration of knightly ceremonial, tournaments at the Louvre, the details of a new Crusade which he was planning, and the distribution of new titles, these were the things occupying the mind of the king, while his kingdom, rent by factions within, was in a death-struggle with foes from without.

A fantastic Don Quixote, on a tottering throne, was fighting the most practical statesman and the strongest-armed warrior Europe held at the time.

With this weakness at the centre, France was again falling into fragments. There was even a resumption of private wars between nobles; and, most paralyzing of all, an empty treasury. Such time as he could spare from his main projects John gave to the affairs of the kingdom. First of all, taxes must be levied; and when the first tax was upon salt, King Edward condescended to make an historic witticism, saying "he had at last discovered who was the author of the Salic Law' "

In the various plans for raising money, it was important that the taxes should be levied so that the burden would fall upon those who could, and who would, pay. This meant the dwellers in the towns and cities: the bourgeoisie. They were the capitalists. But what if they should refuse? In order to secure the success of the measure, it was considered wise to obtain their consent in advance.

When King John asked permission of the States-General to tax them, a critical line was passed. That body for the first time realized its power. It might make its own terms. It demanded that the moneys collected, and their expenditure, should be under the direction of its officers. Then, growing bolder, it demanded reforms: Private wars must cease; the meetings of the States-General must be at appointed intervals, without being summoned by the king.

These meetings at Paris grew stormy. Gradually re-enforced with a vicious element, they were soon led by demagogues, became violent and revolutionary, and finally red caps and barricades, characteristic of Parisian mobs of a later period, brought the whole movement into the hands of the agents of "Charles the Bad," evil genius of his time, who saw his opportunity to use it in his own ambitious designs upon the throne. But France was to hear from the Tiers État again!

In 1356, Edward's son, the Black Prince, won a still greater victory than Crécy, at ***Poitiers,*** in which king John was captured and carried to London.

But Edward found that, while victories were comparatively easy, conquest was difficult. A generation had passed since the war began. So in 1360 both kingdoms were ready to consider terms of peace. By the treaty of Bretigny, Edward renounced the claim to the French throne, and received in full sovereignty the great inheritance Queen Eleanor had brought to Henry II. King John was to be released and his son held as hostage until the enormous ransom was paid. Of course the money could not be paid by impoverished France, for such a doubtful benefit, at least; and so the son and hostage made his escape. Then King John, faithful to his chivalrous creed, returned to London and captivity, dying in 1364.

The dauphin, who had now become Charles V., came to the throne with the determination of restoring France to herself. His attention had been drawn to the military talents of a Breton youth—Bertrand du Guesclin. Poor, diminutive in stature, deformed, he had raised himself to military positions usually reserved as a reward for sons of nobles. In the reopening of a war with England, which Charles was planning, du Guesclin was to be the sword and he the brain.

The Black Prince had gone to Spain to fight the battles of Peter the Cruel, in a civil war in which the Prince was involved by inheritance, and was levying taxes for this Castilian war upon his new subjects in Aquitaine. The people in this province turned to Charles to deliver them from this oppression. He immediately summoned Prince Edward before the Court of Peers; to which the Black Prince replied that he would accept the invitation, but would come with his helmet on his head and sixty thousand men in his party.

So successfully did Charles and du Guesclin meet this renewal of the war that Prince Edward and his sixty thousand men were gradually driven north until the English possessions were reduced to a few towns upon the coast. The Black Prince, under the weight of responsibility and defeat, succumbed to disease, and died, 1377. The death of Edward III. occurred soon after that of his son, and Richard II. was King of England.

The expulsion of the English was not the only benefit bestowed by Charles V. The revolting States-General were restrained and were firmly held in the king's hand. Still more important was the reorganization of the military system, by placing it under the command of officers appointed by the Crown, who might or might not belong to the order of nobility. No more effective blow could have been aimed at feudalism, which was nothing if not militant. Indeed, every act of this brief reign was a protest against the purposes and ideals of his father, King John, who was the embodiment of the ancient spirit. It was a needed breathing-spell between a half-century of disaster behind and another half-century of still greater disaster before.

The death of Charles V. (1380) left the throne to a delicate boy of twelve years, who was to reign under the successive regencies of three uncles. These brothers of Charles, and sons of the romantic King John, seem to represent all the traits and passions which can degrade humanity. The oldest, the Duke of Anjou, was driven from the regency after stealing everything which was movable in the king's palace and vaults. The Duke of Burgundy, who succeeded him, had nobler objects, and needed a larger field for his ambitious soul. He had an eye on the throne itself. And when he and the Duke Berri, at the instigation of the archbishop, were compelled to resign the reins to the young King Charles VI., they carried with them to their own castles all that Anjou had left. Of course the archbishop was mysteriously murdered, and then the boy king was married to Isabella of Bavaria, said to be the most beautiful and the wickedest woman in Europe.

Charles had always been a frail, delicate boy. As he was riding one evening, a strange, wild-looking being sprang out of the darkness and seized the bridle of his horse, crying, "Fly, fly! you are betrayed." The astonished youth after the shock, became melancholy; then was suddenly seized with a fit of frenzy, in which he killed four of his pages. A mad king was on the throne of France, the worst woman in Europe regent, and three uncles waiting like vultures around a dying man, ready to seize anything from a golden candlestick to a throne!

In the chaos of misrule and villainy into which France was falling, the determining factor was the deadly feud which existed between the house of Burgundy and that of Orleans. Upon the death of the first Duke of Burgundy, his son John seized the regency for himself, snatching it from the Duke of Orleans, the king's brother. At this point started the feud which was to tear France asunder from end to end. While the Orleanists were gathering their adherents to drive him out, John was intrenching himself in Paris. Like many another villain, this Duke of Burgundy posed as the friend of the people. He could doff his cap and speak smilingly to starving men. He knew how to work upon their passions, and to please by torturing and executing those they believed had wronged them. He told them how he pitied them for the extortions of the Duke of Orleans and Queen Isabella, kindly giving them pikes to defend themselves, and iron chains to barricade their streets, if they should be needed. Then, extending his hand to his enemy of Orleans, brother of the king, they were reconciled: the past was to be buried.

Then it is a pleasant picture we behold of the period: the two friends partaking together of communion, and dining, and then embracing at parting with effusive words and promises to meet at a dance on the morrow, the unsuspecting Duke of Orleans going out into the dark, where hired assassins were waiting to hack him in pieces. Then a court of justice trying and acquitting this confessed murderer of the king's brother, upon the ground that tyrannicide is a duty; the sad, crazed wraith of a king saying the words he had been taught: "Fair cousin, we pardon you all." And the tragedy and comedy were over!

There was now no check upon the Burgundian power. In the worst days of English occupation of her land, France had been in less danger from Edward III.

than she now was from the Duke of Burgundy, champion and defender of the people! The immediate object of the Burgundian or people's party, and the Orleans and aristocratic party, was the possession of the person of the king, and control of his acts during his few lucid moments.

There was civil war in a land divested of every vestige of government. England would have been blind had she not seen her opportunity; but, too much occupied with her own revolution, she had to wait. And when Henry IV., the first Lancastrian, was king, he needed both hands to hold his crown firmly on his head. But when the young Henry V. came to the throne, with the energy and ambition of youth, the time was ripe for the recovery of the lost possessions in France.

The battle of Agincourt (1415) reopened the war with a great defeat for the French chivalry, which represented the Orleanist party. The wholesale slaughter of princes, bishops, and knights on this fatal day was clear gain for the traitor Burgundy, the champion of the people! The climax of his villainy was at hand.

Henry V., at Rouen, was openly holding his court as King of France. John, Duke of Burgundy, accompanied by Queen Isabella, presented himself to the invading king, and formally pledged his support and that of his followers to the cause of the English!

The infamous treaty of Troyes was signed, 1420. It provided that Henry should act as regent to Charles VI. while he lived; that upon the death of that unhappy being he should be Henry V. of England and Henry II. of France; and that the two kingdoms should thereafter exist under one crown. The romantic marriage of Henry with the Princess Katharine, daughter of Charles and Isabella, which was part of the agreement, was solemnized in that old palace on the island in the Seine. And the same vaulted ceilings which we may see to-day, looked down upon this historic marriage, as they also did upon the condemnation of Marie Antoinette, three and a half centuries later. We know of this union of Henry and the fair Katharine chiefly through the pen of Shakespeare, in his play of Henry V.

But Henry was destined never to wear the crown of France, nor even to see his own land again. There were only two more years of life for him. His death occurred in his palace of the Louvre, a few weeks before that of Charles VI., and the crown he expected to wear upon this event passed to his infant son, who was by the Burgundian party recognized as King of France.

A careless, pleasure-loving dauphin, just twenty, apparently indifferent to the loss of a kingdom, was a frail support at such a time. Only a fragment of the country was held by his followers, the Orleanists; Scotland had come to his aid with a few thousand men, but what did this avail with the greater part of the kingdom held by the Burgundians, while town after town was declaring its allegiance to the English Duke of Bedford, whom his dying brother, Henry V., had named as regent for his infant son.

The city of Orleans, held by the dauphin's adherents, was besieged. It was the key to the situation. Its fall meant the fall of the kingdom, the conquest of France. When this happened, that infant at the Louvre would really be the wearer of the crown. So hopeless was the situation that the spiritless Charles was only in doubt whether to take refuge in Scotland or in Spain.

But although towns and cities had deserted him, the heart of the people had not. Patriotism, dead everywhere else, still lived in the heart of that forgotten multitude lying silent and humble under the feet of its masters. The monarchy had been their friend, their only friend. The Church had deserted them, and joined their enemies the nobles. But to the people, the name King expressed gratitude and hope; and they loved it.

If a great spreading tree full of verdure had arisen in a day out of the barren breast of Mother Earth, it would scarcely have been a greater miracle that what really happened when a child of the soil, a girl, rising triumphant over the disabilities of age, sex, birth, and condition, saved France from destruction. Summoned by celestial voices, by angels whom she not only heard but saw, Joan of Arc started upon her mission of rescue for France!

When this daughter of the people, this peasant from Domremy, was admitted to the presence of the dauphin, it is said that in amusement and in order to test the reality of her mission, Charles exchanged dress with one of his courtiers. But the maid going straight to him, said: "Gentle dauphin, I come to restore to you the crown of France. Orleans shall be saved by me. And you, by the help of God and my Lady St. Catharine, shall be crowned at Rheims."

On the 29th of April the maid did enter the fainting city. And she did lead the dauphin to Rheims for his coronation. And then, kneeling at his feet, asked the "Gentle King" to let her go back to her sheep at Domremy. "For," she said, "they love me more than these thousands of people I have seen."

Unhappily, she did not return to her sheep, but remained among those wolves, and was captured and a prisoner of the English.

What should they do with this strange being, claiming supernatural powers? The Regent Duke of Bedford denounced her as a rebel against the infant king; and the Bishop of Beauvais as a blasphemer and child of the devil. Nothing could be clearer than her guilt upon both of these charges! And on the 13th of May, 1431, this mysteriously inspired child was burnt by a slow fire in the market-place of Rouen. And the "Gentle King," where was he while this was happening?

It must ever remain a mystery that a peasant girl, a child in years and in experience, should have believed herself called to such a mission; that conferring only with her heavenly guides, or "voices," she should have sought the king, inspired him with faith in her, and in himself and his cause, reanimated the courage of the army, and led it herself to victory absolute and complete; and then, have compelled the half-reluctant, half-doubting Charles to go with her to Rheims, there to be anointed and consecrated; this simple child in that day bestowing upon him a kingdom, and upon France a king!

Was there ever a stranger chapter in history! Alas, if it could have ended here, and she could have gone back to her mother and her spinning and her simple pleasures, as she was always longing to do when her work should be done. But no! we see her falling into the hands of the defeated and revengeful English—this child, who had wrested from them a kingdom already in their grasp. She was turned over to the French ecclesiastical court to be tried. A sorceress and a blasphemer they pronounce her, and pass her on to the secular authorities, and her sentence is—death.

We see the poor defenceless girl, bewildered, terrified, wringing her hands and declaring her innocence as she rides to execution. God and man had abandoned her. No heavenly voice spoke, no miracle intervened as her young limbs were tied to the stake and the fagots and straw piled up about her. The torch was applied, and her pure soul mounted heavenward in a column of flames.

Rugged men wept. A Burgundian general said, as he turned gloomily away, "We have murdered a saint."

And Charles, sitting upon the throne she had rescued for him, what was he doing to save her? Nothing—to his everlasting shame be it said, nothing. He might not have succeeded; the effort at rescue, or to stay the event, might have been un-availing. But where was his knighthood, where his manhood, that he did not try, or utter passionate protest against her fate?

Twenty-five years later we see him erecting statues to her memory, and "reha-bilitating" her desecrated name. And to-day, the Church which condemned her for blasphemy is placing her upon the calendar of saints.

CHAPTER X.

CHARLES VII. in creating a standing army struck feudalism a deadly blow. His son, Louis XI., with cold-blooded brutality finished the work. This man's pow-erful and crafty intelligence saw in an alliance with the common people a means of absorbing to himself supreme power. Not since Tiberius had there been a more blood-thirsty monster on a throne. But he demolished the political structure of mediævalism in his kingdom; and when his cruel reign was ended the Middle Ages had passed away, and modern life had begun in France.

There was no longer even the pretence of knightly virtues in France. It was time for the high-born robbers and ruffians in steel helmets to give place to men with hearts and brains. It is said that of those thousands, that chivalric host, which was slaughtered at Agincourt, not one in twenty could write his name. All alike were cruel and had the instincts of barbarians. While the Duke of Burgundy, the richest prince in Europe, was starving his enemies in secret dungeons in the Bas-tille, his Orleans rival, Count of Armagnac, not having access to the Bastille, was decapitating Burgundians till his executioners fainted from fatigue.

It is almost with relief that we read of the slaughter of these knightly savages at Agincourt. If the shipwreck of a mighty kingdom was to be averted, two things must be done. The decaying corpse of feudalism must be thrown overboard, and the Church must be purified. Both had fallen from the ideals which created them; the ideal of truth, justice, and spotless honor, and the ideal of divine love and mercy. Even the semblance of truth and justice and honor had departed from the one; and unspeakable corruption had crept into the other. From the day of the Albigensian cruelties, the heart of the Church had turned to stone, and the spark of life divine within seemed extinguished. Once the guardian of the helpless, it had deserted the people and made common cause with their oppressors. One pope at Rome, and another at Avignon, was a heavy burden to carry. But when *three* infallible beings were hurling anathemas at each other, the University of Paris led Christendom in rejecting them all.

So the two great classes for which the State existed were overweighting the ship at a time when it was being torn and tossed by a storm of gigantic proportions.

Well was it for France that Charles VII., as king, developed unexpected firmness and ability. The creation of a standing army, and the disbanding of all military organizations existing without the king's commission, at one sweeping blow completed the wreck of feudalism. It only remained for Charles's cold-blooded son, Louis XI., to finish the work, and mediævalism was a thing of the past in France.

The reign of Charles was imbittered by the conduct of this unnatural son, whose undisguised impatience to assume the crown so alarmed him that it is said he shortened his own life by abstaining from food in the fear that the dauphin might lay the guilt of parricide upon his soul.

This heart-broken, desolate old man died in 1461. And Louis XI. was King of France.

The son of Charles VII. was a composite of the wisest and the worst of his predecessors. Indeed, it is to the Roman emperors we must look for a parallel to this monster on a throne. And yet, to no other king does France owe such a debt of gratitude. His remorseless hand placed a great gulf between the new and the old, in which were forever buried the men and the system which had fed upon her life.

The antagonism between the son and the father aroused great hopes of a reversal of policy and a rehabilitation of feudalism. These hopes were soon undeceived. So inscrutable and so tortuous was the policy of this strange being, so unexpected his changes of direction, so false and inconsistent his words and acts, and so unspeakably cruel the means to his ends, that a cowed and bewildered nation was soon crouching at his feet, not knowing whither he was leading them.

Warfare played no part in this reign. Invasion was met by diplomacy, and slaughter and bloodshed were relegated to the executioner. Incredible as it seems, it is said that from his windows this king could look out upon an avenue of gibbets upon which hung the bodies of his enemies. The humorous spirit in which he disposed of obstructive nobles is illustrated by a note to an unsuspecting victim. "Fair cousin, come and give us your advice. We have need of so wise a head as yours." And in the morning the fair cousin's wise head was in a basket filled with sawdust!

When all was done, a town council meant more than the "Order of the Golden Fleece"; and, *pari passu,* with the humiliation of the noble came the elevation of the bourgeois. A nameless adventurer would be admitted to confidential intimacy when a Montmorenci could not get beyond his antechamber.

In fact, this levelling up and levelling down was the object of all this king's odious crimes and the central purpose of his cold-blooded reign. If a patent of nobility was a pretty good passport to the scaffold, good service in a town council was an open door to elevation.

So, judged by results, Louis XI. was a better king than many a better man had been. He buried the ideals of the past fathoms deep and then stamped them down with remorseless feet. He demolished the political structure of mediævalism in his kingdom, and when his terrible reign was ended, in 1483, the Middle Ages had passed away and modern life had begun in France.

Almost any reign would have seemed colorless after that of Louis XI. But that of his son, Charles VIII., was made memorable by one event, an invasion of Italy, which brought to France a long train of disastrous consequences.

It will be remembered that in the thirteenth century, Charles, Duke of Anjou, of Sicilian fame, or infamy, and brother of Louis the Saint, occupied the throne of Naples by invitation of the pope.

The family of Anjou having recently become extinct, Charles was now the rightful heir to that throne. So as there was nothing in especial for him to do at home, and as his new army, created and equipped by his father, was a very splendid affair for that day, and as Charles was young and ambitious of a name, he determined to take forcible possession of his inheritance in Italy.

The success of the enterprise was quite dazzling. Milan, Florence, Rome, were successively occupied, and finally Charles was actually seated upon the throne in Naples (1495).

But the seat was not comfortable. The Neapolitans did not want him; and, what was more important, Spain, England, and Austria talked of uniting to drive him out. And so he and his army returned to France, and all that had been gained by the enterprise was a wide-open door between France and Italy at the very time when it might better have been kept closed, and the discovery by Europe that the Italian peninsula was an easy prey to any ambitious European power. What Charles had done might also, and more effectually, be done by England, Spain, or Austria. All of which bore bitter fruit in the next century.

But for France the fruit was of a more deadly kind. The princely and noble blood of Italy began to be mingled with hers, bringing a vicious and corrupt strain at a critical period.

Old as she was in centuries, France was but a child in civilization. An uncouth, untutored child, just emerging from barbarism, was suddenly brought under the influence of a fascinating, highly developed civilization, old in wickedness. A nation in which the ruling class had only recently learned to read and write was naturally dazzled by this sister nation, saturated with the learning and culture of the ages, mistress of every brilliant art and accomplishment; who after having run the whole gamut of human experience, drunk at every known fountain, had arrived at the code summed up by Machiavelli as the best by which to live! It was an easy task for the Medici to control the policy, as they did for generations, of such simple barbarians.

Italy presents a strange spectacle in this closing fifteenth century: All the concentrated splendor from the fall of Byzantium hanging over her like a luminous cloud before dispersing as the Renaissance; Lorenzo de' Medici, at Florence, directing the intellectual currents of Europe; Angelo and Raphael creating the world's sublimest masterpieces in art; her great Genoese son uncovering another hemisphere; Savonarola, like an inspired prophet of old, calling upon men to "repent, repent, while there is yet time"; Machiavelli instructing the nations of the earth in villainy as a fine art; and Alexander VI., the basest man in Europe, poisoner, father of every crime, claiming to be Vicegerent of Christ upon earth!

But the currents were moving swiftly toward a crisis which was to change all this. One more pope, that magnificent patron of art, Julius II., creator of the Vatican Museum, with the recently found Apollo Belvedere, and the Laocoön as a splendid nucleus, and projector and builder of St. Peter's. And then Leo X. (Medicean Pope) and Luther!

The year 1492 contained three important events: the discovery of a new world, the expulsion of the Moors from Spain, and the death of Lorenzo de' Medici. Spain's crusade of seven hundred years was over. We must search in vain for any struggle to match this in singleness and persistence of purpose. Commencing one hundred years before Charlemagne created a Holy Roman Empire, it ended triumphantly under a king and queen who were to play a leading part in the **Reformation.**

The stage was making ready, and the characters were assembling for the great modern drama, in a century even more significant than the one then closing.

The reign of Charles VIII. ended in 1498. And as he left no son, the succession once more passed to a collateral branch: Louis XII., of the House of Orleans, wore the crown of France. It is interesting to recall that these two kings, Charles and Louis, were respectively grandsons of those two ambitious dukes whose personal feud brought France to the verge of ruin a few decades earlier: Louis XII. being the descendant of that Duke of Orleans, brother of Charles VI., the reigning king, who was murdered in the streets of Paris; while Charles VIII. was the descendant of his slayer, the terrible Duke of Burgundy, evil genius of France at that time.

The principal event in the reign of the new king was the reopening of the Italian War by the combined and successful action of Spain and France. But this proved a barren triumph for Louis, who, when all was done, found that he had been simply aiding that artful diplomatist, Ferdinand, in securing the whole prize for Spain. The disagreement growing out of the distribution of the spoil resulted in a war between the late allies; and it was in this wretched conflict that Bayard, *chevalier sans peur et sans reproche,* was sacrificed.

Louis died in 1515, also without an heir; and so the crown passed to still another collateral branch of the main Capetian line. The Count of Angoulême, cousin of the dead king, was proclaimed Francis I.

The fall of Constantinople in the East, and the discovery of a new world in the West, were changing the whole aspect of Europe. The art of printing, coming almost simultaneously with these transforming events, sent vitalizing currents reaching even to the humblest. France partook of the general awakening and was throwing off the torpor of centuries. New ambitions were aroused, and her slumbering genius began to be stirred. This was a propitious moment for an ambitious young king who aimed not only at being the greatest of military heroes, but also the splendid patron of art and letters, and wisest of men! The rôle he had set for himself being, in fact, a Charlemagne and a Lorenzo de' Medici in one. All that was needed for success in this large field was ability. Personal valor Francis certainly possessed. His reign opened brilliantly with a campaign in the Italian peninsula, which left him after the battle of Marignano, master of the Milanese and of northern Italy. He need not trouble himself as had his predecessors about recalcitrant and scheming nobles. They had never been heard from since Louis XI. took them in hand. Neither were the States-General going to annoy him by assertion of rights and demands for reforms. They too had become almost non-existent; it having been well established that only the direst emergency would ever call them into being again. So kingship held sole and undisputed sway, and Francis was looking about to see where he might make it even stronger.

The residence of the popes, at Avignon, during the period of the Great Schism, had led to the establishment by Charles VII. of an ordinance called the ***Pragmatic Sanction;*** its object being the limitation of the papal power in France. The pope by this ordinance was cut off from certain lucrative sources of income; to offset which the king was deprived of the right of appointing officers for vacant bishoprics and abbeys.

Francis I. and Leo X. came together, and, after conferring, determined that the Pragmatic Sanction should be repudiated; Leo, because he must increase his revenues, and Francis, because he desired to use appointments to rich vacancies as rewards for his friends. Leo's tastes, as we know, were magnificent, and needed much more money than he could command; a fact which led to grave results, and changed the course of events in the world!

In 1516 Ferdinand I., King of Spain, died, leaving his enormous possessions to his grandson, Charles, a youth not yet twenty. The mother of this boy was Joanna, the insane daughter of Ferdinand and Isabella, who was married to the son and heir of Maxmilian I., Emperor of Germany.

The young Charles, by the death of his father, had already inherited the Netherlands and Flanders; to which by the death of his maternal grandfather there was now added Spain, the kingdom of Naples, Mexico, and Peru. A heavy enough burden, one would think, for young shoulders. But it was to become still heavier. In 1519 his other grandfather, Maximilian I., died, leaving the throne of the empire vacant.

This office by ancient custom, established by Charlemagne, was elective, and theoretically was open to any prince in Europe. But with the seven princes known as electors, with whom rested choice of the successor, hereditary claim had great weight. Europe saw with dismay the imminent creation of an empire greater than that of Charlemagne—an empire which would cover a large part of the map of Europe and of America. For none was this so alarming as for France, which would in fact be enveloped upon almost every side by this giant among the nations. A French king would indeed have been dull and spiritless not to realize the magnitude of the danger, and Francis was neither. There was only a youth of nineteen standing between him and the greatest dignity in Europe. It was not alone an opportunity to save France from this overshadowing power, but to reunite the crowns of France and the empire as originally designed by Charlemagne. No rôle could have better pleased Francis I. He announced himself a claimant for the vacant throne (under the clause opening it to European princes), claiming that his ownership of the adjacent territory of Northern Italy made him the natural successor to the imperial throne.

Then another ambitious young king appeared as another rival claimant, Henry VIII. of England, with his astute Minister Woolsey to fight the diplomatic battles for his master. It was a brilliant game, played by great players for a great stake: Francis lavishly bribing and dazzling by theatrical displays of splendor; Henry arrogant, ostentatious, vain, and Charles silent, inscrutable, cold-blooded, and false, whispering to Woolsey that he might make him pope at the next election. From that moment the powerful influence of the Cardinal was used for this sedate youth, this wise youth, who saw that the fitting place for him (Woolsey) was the chair of St. Peter!

The diplomacy of the boy of nineteen won the prize. The electors gave the crown to Charles V. Leo X. died soon after. Woolsey waited in hourly expectation of the summons to Rome. But it never came!

Then Francis resolved to win by force what he had lost by diplomacy. Charles succeeded in winning the pope to his side of the contest with the purpose of driving the French out of Italy. The attempt quickly ended in the defeat of the French, and for Francis capture, and a year's imprisonment in Madrid; his release only obtained by abandoning all claims upon Italy; and in 1547 the showy and ineffectual reign of Francis I. was terminated by his death, which occurred almost immediately after that of Henry VIII. in England.

While these events were taking place, a less conspicuous but vastly more significant conflict had developed. In 1517, Martin Luther, the obscure monk, had hurled defiance at the Church of Rome, arraigning Leo X. for corrupt practices; especially the enrichment of the Church by the sale of indulgences. Germany was shaken to its centre by Protestantism, and the reign of Charles V. was to be spent in ineffectual conflict with the Reformation, which would ultimately tear the Empire asunder.

The new heresy had found congenial soil in France. England was openly and avowedly Protestant, while Spain and Italy remained unchangeably Catholic.

For Francis, destined to spend his life in fruitless contest with the more able, wily, and astute Charles V., the religious question upon which Europe was divided meant nothing except at he could use it in his duel with the emperor. He was in turn the ally of Henry VIII. or the willing tool of Charles V. If he needed the English king's friendship, the Protestants had protection. If he desired to placate Charles V., the roastings and torturings commenced again.

In 1547 Francis and Henry VIII. each went to his reward, and a few years later Charles V. had laid down his crown and carried his weary, unsatisfied heart to St. Yuste. The brilliant pageant was over; but Protestantism was expanding.

CHAPTER XI.

THE conversion of Henry VIII., because the pope refused to annul his marriage with Catharine, aunt of Charles V., was not the proudest, but one of the most important triumphs of the new faith. Had Catharine's charms been fresher, or Anne Boleyn less alluring, the course of history would have been changed. Henry VIII., as persecutor of heretics, would have found congenial occupation for his ferocious instincts, and the triumph of Protestantism would have been long delayed. But no such cause existed for the success of the Reformation on French soil. The slumbering germs of heresy, left perhaps by Abelard, or by the heretics in Toulouse and Provence, were quickly warmed into life. It may be also that the memory of her desertion by the Church, once her only friend and champion, gave such intensity to the welcome of a "Reformation" by the people. At all events, whatever the explanation, a religious war was at hand which was going to stain the fair name of France more even than the treacheries of her civil war.

The question at issue was deeper than any one knew. Neither Luther nor Leo X. understood the revolution they had precipitated. Protestants and Papists alike failed to comprehend the true nature of the struggle, which was not for supremacy of Romanist or Protestant; not whether this dogma or that was true, and should prevail; but an assertion of the right of every human soul to choose its own faith and form of worship. The great battle for human liberty had commenced; the struggle for religious liberty was but the prelude to what was to follow. There was abundant proof later that Protestants no less than Papists needed only opportunity and power to be as cruel and intolerant as their persecutors had been. Before the Reformation was fifty years old, Servetus, one of the greatest men of his age, a scholar, philosopher, and man of irreproachable character, was burned at Geneva for heretical views concerning the nature of the Trinity; Calvin, the great organizer of Protestant theology, giving, if not the order for this odious crime, at least the nod of approval for its commission.

France had known many tragedies. But when Francis, in pursuance of his Italian policy, secured the hand of Catharine de' Medici for his son and heir, Henry II., he prepared the way for the most tragic event in her history. Powerless to win the affection, or even confidence, of Henry while he lived, Catharine remained unobserved; but, as the event proved, not unobservant. Her astute mind had been studying every current in the kingdom.

Two families had come into prominence during this reign which were to play leading parts in the immediate future: the family of Guise, of the house of Lorraine, represented by Francis, Duke of Guise; and that of Châtillon, of which Admiral Coligny was the head, both of whom Catharine hated and had marked for destruction.

Mary, of the house of Guise, was the wife of James VI. of Scotland; and through the powerful influence of the Guises, the brothers of the Scottish queen, a marriage was arranged between her daughter—her most serene little highness, Marie Stuart—and the dauphin, who would some day be Francis II.

In order to be prepared for this high destiny, the little maid when only five years old was brought to the Court of France to be trained under the direct influence of the accomplished queen-mother, Catharine—undoubtedly, although unsuspected then, the worst woman in Europe! Poor little Marie Stuart, predestined to sin and to tragedy! What could be expected of a woman with the blood of the Guises in her veins, and with Catharine de' Medici as her model and teacher?

In 1559 Henry II. was killed by an accident at a tournament. The marriage of the two children had taken place. The sickly boy, with only a modest portion of intelligence, was Francis II., King of France. Marie, his beautiful and adored queen, controlled him utterly, and was herself in turn controlled by her uncles of the house of Guise. In fact, the family of Guise, which was the head of the Catholic party in the kingdom, ruled France, with the strange result that if Catharine looked for any allies in her fight with this ambitious family, she must make common cause with the Protestants, led by Admiral Coligny, whom she hated only a little less than the uncles of Marie Stuart.

The princes of the house of Bourbon, a remote branch of the royal family, which, next to Francis, were the nearest to the throne, had been extremely jealous of the growing power of the Guises. Now they saw them, as the advisers of the young king, actually usurping the position which was theirs by right of birth.

Two factions grew out of this feud in the court, and there developed a Bourbon party, and the party of the Guises; one identified with the Protestant and the other with the Catholic cause.

Antony de Bourbon, the head of the family of this name, whether from conviction or from antagonism to the Guises, had openly espoused the Protestant side. It was the rich burghers of the towns, in combination with the smaller nobles, which composed the Protestant party in France. And although the impelling cause of the great movement was religious, political wrongs had become a powerful contributing cause; as is always the case, the discontented and aggrieved, for whatever reason, casting in their lot with those who had a deeper grievance and a more sacred purpose.

Whether the conversion of the Bourbon prince was of that nature or not, who can say? But the movement swelled, and France was divided into two hostile camps: one under the Protestant banner of Antony de Bourbon, father of Henry of Navarre, and the other under that of the Catholic, Francis, Duke of Guise; and two children were on the throne of France while the ground was trembling beneath their feet with a coming revolution.

Francis I. had been too much occupied with his own plans to take in hand systematically and seriously the prevailing heresy. Henry II., son of Francis, had also temporized with the religious revolt, probably not realizing the powerful element it contained. Now, with the Guises firmly in power, there would be no more half-way measures.

But a crisis was at hand which would change the whole situation. The discovery of a plot to seize the person of the young king and place a Bourbon prince upon the throne, led to a general slaughter. Fresh relays of executioners in Paris stood ready to relieve each other when exhausted, and the Seine was black with the bodies of the drowned.

During this preliminary storm the frail young king, Francis II., suddenly died. Marie Stuart passed out of French history, and the power of the Guises was at an end. The fates were certainly fighting on the side of Catharine.

There are hints that the fine Italian hand may be seen in this event which at one stroke removed every obstacle from her path! However this may be, Catharine wasted no regrets upon the death of a son which made her queen regent during the minority of her second son, Charles, now ten years of age (1560).

There was no time to lose. Her control over the feeble Charles IX. before he reached his majority must be absolute. Every impulse toward mercy must be extinguished.

What can be said of a mother who seeks to exterminate every germ of truth or virtue in her son; who immerses him in degrading vices in order to deaden his too sensitive conscience and make him a willing tool for her purposes? Inheriting the splendid intelligence as well as genius for statecraft of the Medici, nourished from her infancy upon Machiavellian principles, cold and cruel by nature, this Florentine woman has written her name in blood across the pages of French history.

There were two main ends to be kept in view: the destruction of the Guises, and the extermination of the Huguenots, as the Protestants were now called. These were difficult to reconcile, but both must be accomplished.

Coligny, the splendid old admiral and Huguenot, hero of the nation, he, too, must go. And Henry of Navarre, the adored young leader of the Huguenots, of course was high on the list marked for destruction; but there might be other uses for him before that time.

Never had the Huguenots received such gentle treatment. Disabilities were removed and privileges bestowed. Never was the beautiful queen-mother as smiling, gracious, and witty. A letter to her uncle, Pope Innocent III., written, it is said, between a dinner and a masquerade, asked if men might not be good enough Christians even if they did not believe in transubstantiation, and useful subjects even though they could not accept the Apostolic succession!

Then this excellent woman declared her admiration for the intelligence of the Huguenots, whom until now she had believed were mere fanatical enthusiasts. Then Henry of Navarre, the brave, generous, accomplished Protestant leader, was urgently invited to the court, and finally even offered the hand of Margaret of Valois, her daughter, as a compromise which would heal the rivalry between the two faiths.

And so, on the 18th of August, 1572, Notre Dame, grim but splendid, looked down upon the marriage of Margaret and Henry, in the presence of all the leaders of Huguenot and Catholic in France.

The Protestants wept for joy at the reconciliation accomplished by this union. And all were to remain and partake of the week of festivities which were to follow.

Then, the pageant over, a secret council was held in Catharine's apartment in the Louvre, in which her remaining son, Henry, participated, but from which his brother the king was excluded; some wishing to include the Guises in the approaching massacre, some urging that Henry of Navarre be spared, but all agreeing that Coligny must go; it being, in fact, the influence of this magnetic man over the young king which was the danger-point compelling haste and the uncertainty as to what her son might do endangered the success of the whole plot.

Charles, who was now king, was impressible, easily influenced, yet stubborn, intractable, incoherent, passionate, and unreliable; sometimes inclining to the Guises, sometimes to Coligny and the Huguenots, and always submitting at last, after vain struggle, to his imperious mother's will, in her efforts to free him from both. We see in him a weak character, not naturally bad, torn to distraction by the cruel forces about him, who when compelled to yield, as he always did in the end, to that terrible woman, would give way to fits of impotent rage against the fate which allowed him no peace.

The time had arrived when Catharine feared the influence of Coligny more than that of the Guises. Brave, patriotic, magnetic, he had succeeded in winning Charles's consent to declare war against Spain. Philip II. of Spain was Catharine's son-in-law and closest ally. Her entire policy was threatened. At all hazards Coligny must be gotten rid of. The young King of Navarre, adored leader of the Protestants, was a constant menace; he, too, must in some way be disposed of.

There were sinister conferences with Philip of Spain and with his minister, that incarnation of cruelty and of the Inquisition, the Duke of Alva.

To the honor of France it may be said that the initiative, the inception of the horrid deed which was preparing was not French. It was conceived in the brain of either this Italian woman or her Spanish adviser and co-conspirator, the Duke of Alva. We shall never know the inside history of the Massacre of St. Bartholomew. It must ever remain a matter of conjecture just how and when it was planned, but the probabilities point strongly one way.

Charles was to be gradually prepared for it by his mother. By working upon his fears, his suspicions, by stories of plottings against his life and his kingdom, she was to infuriate him; and then, while his rage was at its height, the opportunity for action must be at hand. The marriage of Charles's sister Margaret with the young Protestant leader Henry of Navarre, with its promise of future protection to the Huguenots, was part of the plot. It would lure all the leaders of the cause to Paris. Coligny, Condé, all the heads of the party, were urgently invited to attend the marriage feast which was to inaugurate an era of peace.

Admiral Coligny was requested by Catharine, simply as a measure of protection to the Protestants, to have an additional regiment of guards in Paris, to act in case of any unforeseen violence.

Two days after the marriage, and while the festivities were at their height, an attempt upon the life of the old admiral awoke suspicion and alarm. But Catharine and her son went immediately in person to see the wounded old man, and to express their grief and horror at the event. They commanded that a careful list of the names and abode of every Protestant in Paris be made, in order, as they said, "to take them under their own immediate protection." "My dear father," said the king, "the hurt is yours, the grief is mine."

At that moment the knives were already sharpened, every man instructed in his part in the hideous drama, and the signal for its commencement determined upon. Charles did not know it, but his mother did. She went to her son's room that night, artfully and eloquently pictured the danger he was in, confessed to him that *she* had authorized the attempt upon Coligny, but that it was done because of the admiral's plottings against him, which she had discovered. But the Guises—her enemies and his—they knew it, and would denounce her and the king! The only thing now is to finish the work. He must die.

Charles was in frightful agitation and stubbornly refused. Finally, with an air of offended dignity, she bowed coldly and said to her son, "Sir, will you permit me to withdraw with my daughter from your kingdom?" The wretched Charles was conquered. In a sort of insane fury he exclaimed, "Well, let them kill him, and all the rest of the Huguenots too. See that not one remains to reproach me."

This was more than she had hoped. All was easy now. So eager was she to give the order before a change of mood, that she flew herself to give the signal, fully two hours earlier than was expected. At midnight the tocsin rang out upon the night, and the horror began.

Lulled to a feeling of security by artfully contrived circumstances, husbands, wives, sons, daughters, peacefully sleeping, were awakened to see each other hideously slaughtered.

The stars have looked down upon some terrible scenes in Paris; her stones are not unacquainted with the taste of human blood; but never had there been anything like this. The carnage of battle is merciful compared with it. Shrieking women and children, half-clothed, fleeing from knives already dripping with human blood; frantic mothers shielding the bodies of their children, and wives pleading for the lives of husbands; the living hiding beneath the bodies of the dead.

The cry that ascended to Heaven from Paris that night was the most awful and despairing in the world's history. It was centuries of cruelty crowded into a few hours.

The number slain can never be accurately stated, but it was thousands. Human blood is intoxicating. An orgy set in which laughed at orders to cease. Seven days it continued, and then died out for lack of material. The provinces had caught the contagion, and orders to slay were received and obeyed in all except two, the Governor of Bayonne, to his honor be it told, writing to the king in reply: "Your Majesty has many faithful subjects in Bayonne, but not one executioner."

And where was "his Majesty" while this work was being done? How was it with Catharine? We hear of no regrets, no misgivings; that she was calm, collected, suave, and unfathomable as ever; but that Charles, in a strange, half-frenzied state, was amusing himself by firing from the windows of the palace at the fleeing Huguenots. Had he killed himself in remorse, would it not have been better, instead of lingering two wretched years, a prey to mental tortures and an inscrutable malady, before he died?

Europe was shocked. Christendom averted her face in horror. But at Madrid and Rome there was satisfaction.

Catharine and the Duke of Alva had done their work skilfully, but the result surprised and disappointed them. Tens of thousands of Huguenots were slain, which was well; but many times that number remained, with spirit unbroken, which was *not* well.

They had been too merciful! Why had Henry of Navarre been spared? Had not Alva said, "Take the big fish, and let the small fry go. One salmon is worth more than a thousand frogs."

But Charles considered the matter settled when he uttered those swelling words to Henry of Navarre the day after the massacre: "I mean in future to have one religion in my kingdom. It is the Mass or death."

All the events leading up to that fateful night, August 24, 1572, may never be known. Near the Church of St. Germain d'Auxerrois, which rang out the signal and was mute witness of the horror, has just been erected the statue of the great Coligny, bearing the above date.

The miserable Charles was not quite base enough for the part he had played. Tormented with memories, haggard with remorse, he felt that he was dying. His suspicious eyes turned upon his mother, well versed in poisons, as he knew; and, as he also knew, capable of anything. Was this wasting away the result of a drug? Mind and body gave way under the strain. In 1574, less than two years from the hideous event, Charles IX. was dead.

Catharine's third son now wore the crown of France. In Henry III. she had as pliant an instrument for her will as in the two brothers preceding him; and, like them, his reign was spent in alternating conflict with the Protestants and the Duke of Guise. At last, wearied and exasperated, this half-Italian and altogether conscienceless king quite naturally thought of the stiletto. The old duke, as he entered the king's apartment by invitation, was stricken down by assassins hidden for that purpose.

Henry had not counted on the rebound from that blow. Catholic France was excited to such popular fury against him that he threw himself into the arms of the Protestants, imploring their aid in keeping his crown and his kingdom; and when himself assassinated, a year later, the Valois line had become extinct.

By the Salic Law, Henry of Navarre was King of France. The Bourbon branch had left the parent stem as long ago as the reign of Louis the Saint. But as all the other Capetian branches had disappeared, the right of the plumed knight to the crown was beyond a question. So a Protestant and a Huguenot was King of France.

CHAPTER XII.

AFTER long wandering in strange seas, we come in view of familiar lights and headlands. With the advent of the house of Bourbon, we have grasped a thread which leads directly down to our own time.

The accession of a Protestant king was hailed with delirious joy by the Huguenots, and with corresponding rage by Catholic France. The one looked forward to redressing of wrongs and avenging of injuries; and the other flatly refused submission unless Henry should recant his heresy and become a convert to the true faith.

The new king saw there was no bed of roses preparing for him. After four years of effort to reconcile the irreconcilable, he decided upon his course. He was not called to the throne to rule over Protestant France, nor to be an instrument of vengeance for the Huguenots. He saw that the highest good of the kingdom required not that he should impose upon it either form of belief or worship, but give equal opportunity and privilege to both.

To the consternation of the Huguenots, he announced himself ready to listen to the arguments in favor of the religion of Rome; and it took just five hours of deliberation to convince him of its truth. He declared himself ready to abjure his old faith. Bitter reproaches on the one side and rejoicings on the other greeted this decision. It was not heroic. But many even among the Protestants acknowledged it to be an act of supreme political wisdom.

Peace was restored, and the Edict of Nantes, which quickly followed, proved to his old friends, the Huguenots, that they were not forgotten. The Protestants, with disabilities removed, shared equal privileges with the Catholics throughout the kingdom, and the first victory for religious liberty was splendidly won.

An era of unexampled prosperity dawned. Never had the kingdom been so wisely and beneficently governed. Sincerity, simplicity, and sympathy had taken the place of dissimulation, craft, and cruelty. Uplifting agencies were everywhere at work, reaching even to the peasantry, that forgotten element in the nation.

The formal abjuration of the Protestant faith was made by the King in the Church of St. Denis in 1593. This church also witnessed the marriage of Henry with Marie de' Medici, after his release from her debased relative, Margaret of Valois, daughter of Catharine de' Medici. Henry IV., great although he was, was not above the ordinary weaknesses of humanity, and, captivated by the beauty of Marie, was a willing party to the Italian marriage which was urged upon him, which marriage was the one mistake of a great reign.

It was not to be expected that any minister would rise to the full stature of Henry IV. at this time. But in the Duke of Sully he had a wise and efficient instrument for his plan, which was out of the chaos left by the devastation of thirty years of religious wars, to evolve peace and prosperity; and to create economic conditions upon a foundation insuring growth and permanence.

The royal authority, impaired by the successors of Francis, must first be restored. And to that end all political elements, including the States General, must be held firmly down; and that body, representing the Tiers État, ***was never summoned after France was well in hand by the king who was*** par excellence the friend of the people!

It is the Edict of Nantes which stands preeminent among the events of this reign, and which is Henry's monument in the annals of France. His foreign policy was controlled by a desire to check the preponderance of the Hapsburgs; that being, in fact, the dominant sentiment in Europe at that time. But a remarkable proof of the breadth of his treatment of this subject is the plan he formulated of a European tribunal composed of the five great powers, which should insist upon the mainte-nance of a ***balance of power***—a phrase common enough now, but heard then for the first time; and which had for its immediate purpose the separating of the crown of Spain and the empire, by forbidding their being held by members of the same family, and of course designed as a check upon the Hapsburgs.

This was a pet theory with Henry, and the subject of much discussion with Sully and of negotiation with Elizabeth, Queen of England, at the very time when Philip II. of Spain, in pursuance of a precisely opposite policy, had been moving heaven and earth to bring about a marriage with that extraordinary sister of his dead wife Mary. Henry did not witness the realization of his dream. But time has justified its wisdom, and modern statesmanship has been able to devise no wiser plan than that conceived in the mind of this enlightened king nearly three centuries ago.

How much France lost by Ravaillac's dagger can only be surmised, and when Henry, fatally stricken (1610), was carried dying into the Louvre, a cry of grief arose from Catholic and Protestant alike throughout the kingdom. After a reign of twenty-one years, the sagacious ruler, who had done more than any other to make the country great and happy, was the victim of assassination. And France once more was the sport of a cruel fate which placed her in the hands of a woman and a Medici. Marie, the widow of Henry IV., was appointed regent during the minority of her son Louis aged ten years.

The regency of this woman is a story of cabals and the intrigues of aspiring favorites. If Marie had not the ability of her great kinswoman Catharine, it must be confessed neither had she her darker vices. She was simply intriguing and vulgar, and the willing instrument for designing people cleverer than herself. So powerful was the influence of Eleonora Galigai and her husband, Concini, both Italians like herself, that in that superstitious age it was ascribed to magic. Marie became the mere secretary to record the wishes of these parasites. Concini was made marquis, then minister. Whom he commended was elevated, and whom he denounced was abased. Public indignation reached its climax when this adventurer was finally cre-ated Marshal of France, before whom counts and dukes must bow. So furious was the storm raised by this, that Marie declared her willingness to surrender the regency, and after summoning the States General she presented her son, Louis XIII., thirteen years of age, declaring that he was qualified to reign.

Only once again was this body to be called together. That was in 1789, by Louis XVI., when it was transformed into a National Assembly.

But when it was discovered that the power of the detested pair was as great behind the boy king as it had been behind his mother, the storm gathered again from all parts of the kingdom. It was France in struggle with Concini, the man who was audaciously sending princes of the blood and dukes to the Bastille.

But a counter-influence was weaving about Louis. He was made to realize the indignity to himself in letting two vulgar Italians usurp his authority. Thus Albert de Luynes, his adored friend, procured his signature to a paper ordering the immediate destruction of Concini and his wife. And when Louis had seen Concini despatched by his own agents in the court of the Louvre, and the arrest, trial, and execution of Eleonora (upon the charge of sorcery), he completed the work by banishing his mother, only to fall immediately into the power of Albert de Luynes, himself an intriguing parasite, who intended to play the very same rôle as the pair he had overthrown.

The clever Eleonora, when arraigned on the charge of sorcery, replied, "The only magic I have used is that of a strong mind over a weak one." Albert de Luynes's head was never carried about Paris on a pike, as was hers. But he experimented with the same kind of magic.

This wretched period after the death of the great Henry had occupied twelve years. But in 1622 Cardinal Richelieu took his seat among the advisers of the king. The true man had been found. King, nobles, people of all ranks and religions, realized that a master had appeared in the land; a master inscrutable in his purposes, and clothed with a mysterious power.

The foundations of this man's policy lay deep, out of sight of all save his own far-reaching intelligence. Pitiless as an iceberg, he crushed every obstacle to his purpose. Impartial as fate, with no loves, no hatreds, catholics, protestants, nobles, parliaments, one after another were borne down before his determination to make the king, what he had not been since Charlemagne, supreme in France.

The will of the great minister mowed down like a scythe. The power of the grandees, that last remnant of feudalism, and a perpetual menace to monarchy, was swept away. One great noble after another was humiliated and shorn of his privileges, if not of his head.

The Huguenots, being first shaken into submission, saw their political liberties torn from them by the stroke of a pen; and even while the Catholics were making merry over this discomfiture the minister was planning to send Henrietta, sister of the king, across the channel to become queen of Protestant England, as wife of Charles I. But the act of supreme audacity was to come. This high prelate of the Church, this cardinal-minister, formed an alliance with Gustavus Adolphus, the great leader of the Protestants in the war upon the emperor and the pope!

He allowed no religion, no class, to sway or to hold him. He was for France; and her greatness and glory augmented under his ruthless dominion. By his extraordinary genius he made the reign of a commonplace king one of dazzling splendor; and while gratifying his own colossal ambition, he so strengthened the foundations of the monarchy that princes of the blood themselves could not shake it.

It was great, it was dazzling, but of all his work there is but one thing which revolutions and time have not swept away: the "French Academy" alone survives as his monument. Out of a gathering of literary friends he created a national institution, its object the establishing a court of last appeal in all that makes for eloquence in speaking or writing the French language. In a country where few things endure, this has remained unchanged for two hundred and thirty years.

But this master of statecraft, this creator of despotic monarchy, had one unsatisfied ambition. He would have exchanged all his honors for the ability to write one play like those of Corneille. Hungering for literary distinction, he could not have gotten into his own Academy had he not created it. And jealous of his laurels, he hated Corneille as much as he did the enemies of France.

The feeble King Louis XIII. manifested wisdom in at least one thing. He permitted this greatest statesman of his time, and one of the greatest perhaps of all time, to have a free hand in managing his kingdom. And whatever the pressure from the queen-mother, from cabals and intriguing nobles, he never yielded the point, but kept his great minister in his service as long as they both lived. This was especially commendable in Louis because they were personally antagonistic, and also because the queen-mother constantly used her powerful influence over her son for his downfall.

Marie had been permitted to return to Paris, where her son, perhaps to console her for the loss of the Concinis, had built for her the Palais de Luxembourg, intended as a reminiscence of her dear Italy, with its Medicean architecture and Italian gardens and fountains. Here she held her little court in great splendor, and here she wove her ineffectual webs for Richelieu's defeat and downfall. It is said that at one time Louis at her instigation had actually taken the pen in hand to sign the order for his minister's disgrace, when that vigilant and omniscient being, perfectly aware of what was occurring, appeared from behind the curtains. And Louis, quailing before the superior will of a master, sent his vicious, intriguing mother into perpetual banishment. And we are told that Marie, the subject of those immortal canvases now at the Louvre, was actually sheltered and fed by the great painter at his own home in the day of her disgrace and poverty.

It is not strange that Peter the Great pronounced Richelieu the model statesman! Their ideals were the same. The minister intended that everything in France should lie helpless at the feet of royalty; that kingship should absorb into itself every source of power. While Cromwell was tearing down a throne in England and leading a king to a scaffold, Richelieu, facing every class, current, and force, was making the throne impregnable in France, and preparing a magnificent inheritance for the infant Louis XIV., then in his cradle.

Queen-mother, nobles, parliaments, and Protestants must be taught to obey. The Huguenots at the siege of La Rochelle, lasting fifteen months, learned their lesson. The punishment for their revolt was the loss of every military and political privilege. But although there were to be no more political assemblies, the edict of Nantes was to be rigidly enforced, and their rights and immunities under it made inviolable. Louis the King saw his most intimate friend, Cinq Mars, sent to the scaffold; his brother Gaston, Duke of Orleans, thrown into the Bastille like a common prisoner; his mother in exile and poverty. But he also saw himself without the trouble of governing, surrounded by homage and adulation, towering high above everything else in France, and was content.

The growing power of Austria and the ascendency of the Hapsburgs was, as we have seen, the nightmare of Europe at this period. But the Reformation was tearing the empire almost asunder. A Protestant Prussia was trying to struggle away from a Catholic Austria. Richelieu cared nothing for Catholics nor for Protestants. His aim was to weaken the hands of the Hapsburgs. And if he joined the Protestant leader Gustavus Adolphus in a religious crusade, it was with this end in view.

The marriage of Louis with the Infanta of Spain, known as Anne of Austria, was doubtless a part of the same line of policy, and was the beginning of many attempts to draw the Spanish peninsula under the control of France.

When the end of all these schemings arrived, on the 4th day of December, 1642, Richelieu calmly laid down to die in his princely residence known at that time as the Palais Cardinal. But as it was his dying gift to the king, the name was changed to the Palais Royal. Upon the death of Louis XIII., which occurred in 1643, only a few months after that of his minister, the widowed Queen Anne, with her infant son, Louis XIV., removed from the Louvre to the Palais Royal, which continued to be the residence of the Grand Monarch for some time after his majority.

Anne was appointed regent for her son, not yet five years old, and, to the surprise of everyone, immediately called to her aid as her adviser not a Frenchman, as was expected, but an Italian, Cardinal Mazarin. So the fate of the kingdom was in the hands of two foreigners, a Spanish queen-regent and an Italian minister.

Richelieu's and Mazarin's methods were the opposite of each other. One was direct, the other tortuous and indirect. In true Italian fashion Mazarin overcame by seeming to yield; and what he said was the thing he did not mean. Intrigue and bribery were his implements and weapons.

The situation awoke distrust. It was a time to recover lost privileges, and to struggle out of the chains riveted by Richelieu. A civil war known as the Fronde was the result.

As all classes had grievances, all were represented in this general undoing of the last minister's great work. But as no two classes desired the same thing, the miserable war, without genius and without system, miserably failed. The royal cause triumphed; and Richelieu's political structure was not even shaken. Mazarin stood inflexibly by the work of his great predecessor. Turenne and Condé were the military heroes of this, as well as of the subsequent foreign wars, resulting in the acquisition of Alsace (1648) and other great territorial expansion.

When Cardinal Mazarin died in 1661, the young king was asked to whom the ministers should bring their portfolios. To which came the unexpected reply, *"To me."*

CHAPTER XIII.

THE wily Italian was gone, and Louis XIV. settled himself upon the throne which Richelieu had rendered so exalted and immovable.

Cardinal Mazarin had said of the young Louis that "there was enough in him to make four kings, and one honest man." His greatness consisted more in amplitude than in kind. Nature made him in prodigal mood. He was an average man of colossal proportions. His ability, courage, dignity, industry, greed for power and possessions, were all on a magnificent scale, and so were his vanity, his loves, his cruelties, his pleasures, his triumphs, and his disappointments.

No king more wickedly oppressed France, and none made her more glorious. He made her feared abroad and magnificent at home, but he desolated her, and drained her resources with ambitious wars. He crowned her with imperishable laurels in literature, art, and every manifestation of genius, but he signed the Revocation of the Edict of Nantes, and drove out of his kingdom 500,000 of the best of his subjects.

The marriage of the Dauphin with the Infanta of Spain had occurred before he attained his majority. It was planned by Mazarin, and was a part of the policy left as a fatal bequest to Louis XIV. by that minister.

The Salic Law was not recognized in Spain. Hence, the crown might descend to an heiress, and by her be transmitted to her husband. Such was the hope in the marriage of Louis with the Infanta; the hope of some happy turn of fortune, some break in the line of succession whereby the Spanish kingdom might be absorbed into a Bourbon empire, as it had once been in the empire of the Hapsburgs. This was the *ignis fatuus* which was to control the policy of this stormy reign, and which was to envelop it at last in the clouds of defeat and disaster.

The secret of Louis' greatness was his instinctive recognition of greatness in others. His new minister, Colbert, to whom he owed so much, was a man of the people, and a protestant. He it was who discovered the peculations of Fouquet, the magnificent Minister of Finance, who was building a palace at Vaux greater than the king himself could afford, and who was suddenly swept from this princely residence into the Bastille, where he spent the remaining years of his life with plenty of leisure in which to think upon the forty thousand pounds he had expended upon that fête he gave in honor of his royal master; and to recall the splendors of the supper and the size of the banqueting-hall, which Mansart, Le Brun, and the best that Italy could furnish at that time had made beautiful.

It is said that the unfortunate visit of the king to his minister's abode resulted in the creation of Versailles as a suburban residence. From the Palais de St. Germain, on the heights in the suburbs of Paris, Louis could see the Cathedral of St. Denis, where were the royal vaults and the ancestors he must some day join. So depressing was this view to him, and so charmed was he with the plan of Fouquet's palace and gardens, that artists were immediately set to work to make one more royal at Versailles, where his father, Louis XIII., used to have his hunting-box; the place where that much-governed king used to go to hide away from his scheming mother and his argus-eyed minister. The genius of Colbert was severely taxed to supply the means for Louis' magnificent tastes and for his foreign wars, at the same time. Even Colbert could not create money out of nothing. The burden must rest somewhere, and just as surely must ultimately be borne by the people.

The choice of Louvois as Minister of War was no less happy than that of Colbert in Finance. And with Vauban to build his defences, Turenne and Luxembourg and the great Condé to lead his armies, it is not strange that there were victories.

The four great wars of Louis' reign were not for theatrical effect, like that of the fanciful Charles VIII. in Italy. They were all in pursuance of a serious and definite purpose. Just or unjust, wise or unwise, they were planned in order to reach some boundary, or to secure some strategic position essential to France. These wars were:

First—The war upon the Spanish Netherlands, ending with the Treaty of Aix-la-Chapelle, 1668.

Second—The invasion of the Dutch Republic, ending with the peace of Nymwegen, 1678.

Third—War with the coalition of European States, closing with the Treaty of Ryswick, 1697.

Fourth—War of the Spanish Succession, closed by the Treaty of Utrecht, 1713.

The first of these wars, undertaken because Louis believed and intended that Flanders should belong to France, to which it was geographically allied, was ostensibly undertaken in order to recover the unpaid dowry which had been promised by Spain in exchange for Louis' renunciation of any claim upon the throne of Spain which might result from his marriage with the Infanta Maria Theresa. His conquest of the Spanish possessions in Flanders might have been supposed to set at rest forever the question of a claim upon the Spanish throne. But we shall hear of that again. The success of this war made Louis, at twenty-nine years of age, the most heroic figure in Europe. Every one bowed before him, and everything seemed to be gravitating toward him as toward a central sun. Not alone nobility, but even genius put on his livery and became sycophantish, Bossuet and even Molière, hungering for his smile, and in despair if he frowned.

This was the time of the supremacy of the beautiful Louise la Vallière. Her reign was brief, and, the king's infatuation being passed, she was to spend the rest of her dreary life in a Carmelite convent, hearing only the far-off echoes from the brilliant world in which she was once the central and envied figure.

The Dutch Republic had come under Louis' displeasure and was marked for his next foreign campaign. This (to his mind) insignificant nation of fishermen and small traders had presumed to stand in his path. So the most magnificent army since the Crusades in 1672 invaded the peaceful little state of Holland. As one after another of the cities helplessly fell, someone asked why Louis came himself—why he did not send his valet? Louis insolently demanded as the price of peace the surrender of all their fortified cities, the payment of twenty million francs, and the renunciation of the Protestant faith.

The answer of William of Nassau was an unexpected one. The history of modern times has nothing more heroic than this little mercantile state defying the greatest potentate in Europe. William of Nassau knew perfectly well that every battle meant defeat. The thing to do was to make battles impossible by inundating their fertile fields. When he saw the destruction of life and property in one scale and political slavery in the other, he did not hesitate. The dikes were quietly opened. Turenne and Luxembourg and Vauban were baffled as completely as Napoleon in Russia. And when the magnificent army had evacuated the flooded country, the dikes were quietly closed again and time and windmills restored their fields to fertility.

In the meantime William had been drawing to himself powerful allies. Half of Europe was in league with him in the battles he now fought upon the Rhine. But the French were victorious. And after the peace of Nymwegen, 1678, Louis had reached the zenith of his power.

Human pretension and arrogance could go no farther. He began to feel that France was his own personal possession and that Europe might be. It was the combination of a great king with a small man which produced this composite being. He had built Versailles, a palace unmatched since the Cæsars. He not only commanded the presence, but the obsequious presence of all that was illustrious and great at a time when France was in the full flower of her splendid genius. Corneille, Racine, Molière, if permitted to be, must pay him an almost idolatrous homage. The beautiful Vallière was sent away, and de Montespan's reign had commenced.

But when Colbert died in 1685, Louis fell under an influence which was to be transforming. He had been burning the illuminating oil of youth at very high pressure. Perhaps it was exhausted. He grew serious. De Montespan was sent away—the orgies at Versailles ceased, the court became decorous, almost austere, and with the awakening of conscience, of course, the king became more sensitive to the heresies of the Huguenots!

He was drifting toward the fatal mistake of his life. He revoked the Edict of Nantes. Two millions of people by the stroke of his pen, at the bidding of de Maintenon, were disfranchised; prohibited under severe penalties from any observance of their religion; their property confiscated, an attempt to flee from the country punished by the galleys.

The prisons were full of Protestants and the scaffolds dyed with their blood. Two hundred thousand perished by imprisonment, by the galleys, and the executioner; while two hundred thousand more managed to escape to America and to the lands of the enemies of France, which they would enrich with their skill.

Not a word of protest came from a person in France. Not even from Fénelon or Bossuet! Madame de Maintenon told him it was the "glorious climax of a glorious reign." Madame de Sévigné said it was "magnificent!" And Bossuet, greatest of French divines, exclaimed, "It is the miracle of the century!"

France at one stroke was impoverished. The skill, the trained hand, the element which was at the foundation of her excellence, and of that which was to constitute her future supremacy in the world, had gone to enrich her enemies. And whether in Germany, in England, or America, no foreign people have had such glad welcome as was given to the Huguenots.

Then came the rebound in a form not expected. William of Orange was now King of England. James had been driven off his throne, and his daughter Mary and her husband, William of Orange, wore the double crown. All the hostile European states, under William's leadership, sprang together for the common defence of Europe from this detested foe.

The smothered hatred of Holland and every protestant state burst into flame, and the great War of the Coalition commenced. Beginning with the League of Augsburg, in 1688, it continued until the peace of Ryswick, 1697, with the defeat of France all along the line.

Humiliated and broken, there remained for the king an opportunity to retrieve the past by attaching the Spanish peninsula to France. There was a vacant throne at Madrid which his grandson Philip, through the neglected Queen Maria Theresa, might claim as his inheritance. Such were the conditions which might still change defeat into triumph. The fact that the right to the succession had been waived by the king was easily disposed of. Philip, Louis' grandson, presented his claim in competition with that of the son of Leopold I., Emperor of Germany. When the pope, with whom the decision lay, decided in favor of Philip, grandson of the great Louis, all Europe sprang to the aid of the Austrian archduke in the war of the Spanish succession.

It was a little side play in the opening of this great drama, which brought the kingdom of Prussia into existence. Frederick, elector of Brandenburg, when called upon to arm by the emperor, refused to do so except upon one condition: that he might wear the title of king instead of elector; which condition was granted, with the stipulation that the name of Prussia, a detached piece of territory the ancestors of Frederick had cut out of the side of Russia, be substituted for Brandenburg. So out of this war of personal ambition there had sprung a new kingdom, the kingdom of Prussia, of which France was to hear much in the future.

England was not eager to join the new coalition in defence of the Hapsburg, whom in common with the rest of Europe she had for years been trying to pull down. But when Louis insolently espoused the cause of the exiled King James, and promised by force to place the pretender on the throne, then she needed no urging, and sent Marlborough and the flower of her army to join Prince Eugene in Germany.

It was Marlborough at Blenheim (1702) who drove the iron of defeat into the soul of Louis XIV. When the war was ended he had made every concession demanded; had given up a vast extent of territory; banished the English pretender from his kingdom; and acknowledged Anne as queen of Great Britain.

By the provisions of the treaty (the Peace of Utrecht) Gibraltar passed to England; Spain ceded the Netherlands and all her possessions in Italy to the German empire. And so the fine threads diplomacy had been spinning over the Continent for two centuries were ruthlessly brushed away as a spider's web.

An imbittered, broken old man, shorn of his omnipotence, who had outlived his fame and his worshippers, was dying in his great palace at Versailles; his only solace the austere woman who had inspired the Revocation of the Edict of Nantes, and who upon the death of his unhappy queen he had privately made his wife. Marie Therese had borne his mad infatuation for Louise la Vallière; la Vallière had carried her broken heart to a convent, and been superseded by de Montespan, and de Montespan had invited her own destruction by bringing into her household Madame de Maintenon, the pious widow of the poet Scarron, in order that the austere virtues of that lady might be engrafted upon the children of the royal household. Grave, ambitious, talented, the governess of de Montespan's children was not too much absorbed in her duties to find ways of establishing an influence over the king.

This man, who had absorbed into himself all the functions of the government, who was ministers, magistrates, parliaments, all in one, this central sun of whom Corneille, Molière, Racine were but single rays, was destined to be enslaved in his old age by a designing adventuress; her will his law. The hey-day of youth having passed, he was beginning to be anxious about his soul. She artfully pricked his conscience, and de Montespan was sent away, but de Maintenon remained.

She next convinced him that the only fitting atonement for his sins was to drive heresy out of his kingdom, and re-establish the true faith. At her bidding he undid the glorious work of Henry IV., signed the Revocation of the Edict of Nantes, and brutally stamped out Protestantism.

During the seventeenth and eighteenth centuries the stake in the great game played in Europe was the headship, the pre-eminent position held by the house of Hapsburg. The entire reign of Louis XIV. had had this for its ultimate object. He seemed many times near it; but was never to reach the goal. The absorption of Spain was a last and desperate attempt. It had failed. France had not won the leadership of European civilization.

In the coming reign, new forces, new conditions, were to widen the field of national ambitions. And it was the nation across the channel which would grasp these forces and distance her rivals in an advance along the untried paths of commerce and a world-wide expansion.

With a strange apathy France had seen herself mistress of a large part of the American Continent, won for her by adventurous Frenchmen and Catholic missionaries. She did practically nothing to develop this magnificent colonial empire. Failing to comprehend changing conditions, the same old problem, with a towering house of Hapsburg, obscured her view, and remained the great unchanging fact about which her policy revolved.

Louis XV. was five years old when, in 1715, he became heir to a throne absolutely rigid. The best work of Richelieu and Mazarin and Louis XIV. had been expended upon it. Absolutism could go no farther. The king was all; next below him a fawning, obsequious nobility, and then that vague entity known as "the people," a remote invisible force, sustaining the weight of the splendid pyramid, the apex of which was this boy of five.

The young Louis was being prepared to sit upon this giddy elevation. The Duke of Orleans, his accomplished cousin, a competent instructor in vice, was chosen as regent, and the royal education began. The best and rarest of the world's culture was at his service. Fénelon, the polished ecclesiastic, fed him the classics in tempting form from his own Télémaque, written for the purpose. Although this work was later suppressed by the boy's royal father under the suspicion of being a covert satire upon his own reign, in which Madame de Montespan was represented by Calypso; and other famous or infamous members of his court also appeared in thin disguise.

The handsome boy was breathing the atmosphere of genius created by an age which compares well with those of Pericles and Augustus and the Medici, and nourished at the same time by the exhalations from a new crop of vices growing out of the decaying remains of those left by the old court.

CHAPTER XIV.

SUCH was the preparation for a supreme crisis in the life of the Kingdom.

The enormous debt left by the last reign taxed the ingenuity of the regent to its utmost. Then it was that John Law, the Scotchman, presented his great financial scheme of making unlimited wealth out of paper, which was just what the regent needed. The collapse came quickly, in 1720, bringing ruin to thousands, and leaving the country in more desperate need than before.

When declared of age, in 1723, a marriage was arranged for Louis with Marie Leczinska, daughter of the exiled Polish King Stanislas. Europe at this time was agitated over the succession to the throne of Austria, as the empire was now called. The Salic Law excluded female heirs, and the emperor, Charles VI., had died in 1718, leaving only a daughter, Maria Theresa, one year old. But a pragmatic sanction, once more invoked, seems to have covered the necessities of the situation by providing that the succession in the absence of a male heir might descend to a female, and so there was a young and beautiful empress on the throne at Vienna, who was going to make a great deal of history for Europe; and who would open her brilliant reign by a valiant fight for possession of Silesia, which the young king of Prussia intended to seize as an addition to his own new kingdom. This young King Frederick was also making history very fast, and after a stormy career was going to convert his Kingdom into a Power, and to be the one sovereign of his age whom the world would call *Great!* But at this particular period of his youth, Frederick and his nobility, still blinded by the splendors of the reign of Louis XIV., were mere servile imitators of the court at Versailles, and the culture and the civilization for which they hungered were French—only French; and for Frederick, an intimate companionship with Voltaire was his supreme desire. But a closer view of the witty, cynical Frenchman wrought a wonderful change. The finely pointed shafts of ridicule when aimed at himself were not so entertaining. And his guest, no longer *persona grata,* was escorted over the frontier to France.

A nearer view of Versailles at this time might also have disenchanted these worshippers at the shrine of French civilization. A king absolutely indifferent to conditions in his kingdom, immersed in debasing pleasures, while Madame de Pompadour actually ruled the state—this is not the worst they would have seen! Destitute of shame, of pity, of patriotism, and of human affection, what did it mean to the king that his people were growing desperate under the enormous taxation made necessary by incessant wars and by the extravagant expenditures of the court? Louis simply turned his back upon the whole problem of administration, and left his ministers, Fleury, and later de Choiseul, to deal with the misery and the discontent and to make their way through the financial morass as best they might.

The power of Madame de Pompadour may be imagined when we learn that Maria Theresa, empress and proud daughter of the Cæsars, when she needed the friendship of Louis XIV., in her struggle with Frederick of Prussia, in order to win him to her side, wrote a flattering letter to this woman.

This friendship, so artfully sought by the empress, led to another very different and very momentous alliance. A marriage was arranged between her little daughter, Marie Antoinette, and the boy Louis, who was to be the future king of France. The dauphin, the dauphiness, and their eldest child were all dead. So Louis, the second son of the dauphin, was the heir to his grandfather, Louis XV.

How should the empress of Austria, born, nurtured, and fed in the very centre of despotism, utterly misunderstanding as she must the past, the present, and the future, how should she suspect that the throne of France would be a scaffold for her child? Hapsburg and Bourbon were to her realities as enduring as the Alps.

In the meantime England and France had come into collision over their boundaries in America, and the war opened by Braddock and his young aide, Washington, had been a still further drain upon impoverished France. With the loss of Montreal and Quebec, those two strongholds in the north, the French were virtually defeated. And when the end came, France had lost every inch of territory on the North American Continent, and had ceded her vast possessions, extending from Canada to the Gulf of Mexico, to England and Spain.

So while England was steadily building up a world-empire, penetrated with the forces of a modern age, France, loaded with debt, was taxing a people crying for bread—taxing a starving people for money to procure unimaginable luxuries and pleasures for Madame du Barry, who had succeeded to the place once held by Madame de Pompadour. Did she desire a snowstorm and a sleighride in midsummer, these must be created and made possible. And one may see to-day at Versailles the sleigh in which this mad caprice was realized.

The various instructors of Louis XV. had not taught him anything about mind and soul processes. They were quite unaware that there had commenced a movement in the ***brain*** of France, which was going to liberate terrific forces—forces which would sweep before them the work of the Richelieus and the Mazarins and the Colberts as if it were chaff.

The human mind was probing, questioning, doubting, everything it had once believed. And as one after another cherished beliefs disappeared, it grew still more daring. The whole religious, social, and political system was wrong. The only remedy was to overthrow it all, and crown reason as the sovereign of a new era. Such was the ferment at work beneath the surface as Louis was devising incredible extravagances for du Barry. And there was rage in men's hearts as they wrote insulting lines upon his equestrian statue in the Place Louis Quinze.

The Place Louis Quinze was soon to be the Place de la Révolution. The bronze statue was to be melted into bullets by a maddened populace, and standing on that very spot was to be the guillotine which would destroy king, queen, the king's sister, and a great part of the nobility of France.

It is said that the three great events of modern times are the Reformation, the American War of Independence, and the French Revolution. Events such as these have a lurid background, a long vista of causes behind them! A French Revolution is not the work of a day, nor of a single man. There had been a steady movement toward this event for a thousand years—in fact, ever since the dogma that ***labor is degrading*** was placed at the foundation of the social structure of France.

The direct causes which were precipitating the crisis in the closing eighteenth century were financial and economic, while the contributing causes were a remarkable intellectual movement and the War of Independence in America. It is possible that a king with a heart and a brain, and the moral sense which belongs to ordinary humanity, might have averted this tragic outburst, and at least have delayed the event by awakening hope. The Revolution was born of hopeless misery. With the reign of Louis XV. hope died, and his successor fell heir to the inevitable.

A heartless sybarite, depraved in tastes, without sense of responsibility or com-prehension of his times, a brutalized voluptuary governed by a succession of design-ing women, regardless of national poverty, indulging in wildest extravagance—such was the man in whom was vested the authority rendered so absolute by Richelieu; such the man who opened up a pathway for the storm.

As for the nobility, their degradation may be imagined when it is said there was as bitter rivalry between titled and illustrious fathers to secure for their daughters the coveted position held by Madame de Pompadour, as for the highest offices of State.

Could the upper ranks fall lower than this? Had not the kingdom reached its lowest depths, where its foreign policy was determined by the amount of consid-eration shown to Madame de Pompadour? But this woman, whose friendship was artfully sought by the great Empress Maria Theresa, was superseded, and the fresher charms of Madame du Barry enslaved the king. The deposed favorite could not survive her fall, and died of a broken heart. It is said that as Louis, looking from an upper window of his palace, saw the coffin borne out in a drenching rain, he smiled, and said, "Ah, the marquise has a bad day for her journey." It may be imagined that the man who could be so pitiless to the woman he had loved would feel little pity for the people whom he had not loved, but whom he knew only as a remote, ob-scure something, which held up the weight of his glory.

But this "obscure something" was undergoing strange transformation. The greater light at the surface had sent some glimmering rays down into the mass be-low, which began to awaken and to think. Misery, hopeless and abject, was chang-ing into rage and thirst for vengeance.

A new class had come into existence which was not noble, but with highly trained intelligence it looked with contempt and loathing upon the frivolous, half-educated nobles. Scorn was added to the ferment of human passions beneath the surface, and when Voltaire had spoken, and the restraints of religion were loos-ened, no living hand, not that of a Richelieu nor a Louis XIV., could have averted the coming doom. But no one seems to have suspected what was approaching.

A wonderful literature had come into existence, not stately and classic as in the age preceding, but instinct with a new sort of life. The profoundest themes which can occupy the mind of man were handled with marvellous lightness of touch and clothed with prismatic brilliancy of speech; but all was negation. None tried to build; all to demolish. The black-winged angel of Destruction was hovering over the land.

Then Rousseau tossed his dreamy abstractions into the quivering air, and the formula, "Liberty, Equality, and Fraternity," was caught up by the titled aristocracy as a charming idyllic toy, while princes, dukes, and marquises amused themselves with a dream of Arcadian simplicity, to be attained in some indefinite way, in some remote and equally indefinite future. It was all a masquerade. No reality, no sincerity, no convictions, good or evil. The only thing that was real was that an overtaxed, impoverished people was exasperated and—hungry.

Did the king need new supplies for his unimaginable luxuries, they were taxed. Was it necessary to have new accessions to French "glory," in order to allay popular clamor or discontent, they must supply the men to fight the glorious battles, and the means with which to pay them. Every burden fell at last upon this lowest stratum of the State; the nobility and clergy, while owning two-thirds of the land, being nearly exempt from taxation.

And yet the king and nobility of France, in love with Rousseau's theories, were airily discussing the "rights of man"—wolves and foxes coming together to talk over the sacredness of the rights of property, or the occupants of murderers' row growing eloquent over the sanctity of human life! How incomprehensible that among those quick-witted Frenchmen there seems not one to have realized that the logical sequence of the formula, "Liberty, Equality, and Fraternity," must be, "Down with the Aristocrats!"

And so the surface which Richelieu had converted into adamant grew thinner and thinner each day, until king and court danced upon a mere gilded crust, unconscious of the abysmal fires beneath. Some of those powdered heads fell into the executioner's basket twenty-five years later. Did they recall this time? Did Madame du Barry think of it? Did she exult at her triumph over de Pompadour, when she was dragged shrieking and struggling to the guillotine?

Five years before the close of this miserable reign an event occurred seemingly of small importance to Europe. A child was born in an obscure Italian household. His name was Napoleon Bonaparte. His birthplace, the island of Corsica, had only two months before been incorporated with France. The fates even then were watching over this child of destiny, who might, by a slight turn of events then imminent, have been born a subject of Spain, or Germany, or of George III. of England.

The impoverished Republic of Genoa was in desperate need of money. The island could be had by the highest bidder, and in 1768 it was purchased by France, just in time to make the great Corsican a French citizen.

Indeed, all the performers in the approaching drama were assembled. Three young princes, grandsons of Louis XV., who were to be successively upon the throne of France, were at Versailles: Louis the Dauphin, now twenty, and his Austrian bride, Marie Antoinette, and his two brothers, afterward successively Louis XVIII. and Charles X. Still another princeling, Louis Philippe, was at the Palais Royal, son of the Duke of Orleans, late regent, also destined to wear the French crown; and last of all that infant at Ajaccio, in whom the play was to reach its splendid climax.

In 1744 Louis XV. was stricken with small-pox, and exchanged the brilliant scenes at Versailles for the royal vault in the Church of St. Denis, where he took his place among his ancestors.

CHAPTER XV.

LOUIS XV. was dead, and two children, with the light-heartedness of youth and inexperience, stepped upon the throne which was to be a scaffold—Louis XVI., only twenty, and Marie Antoinette, his wife, nineteen. He, amiable, kind, full of generous intentions; she, beautiful, simple, child-like, and lovely. Instead of a de-bauched old king with depraved surroundings, here were a prince and princess out of a fairy tale. The air was filled with indefinite promise of a new era for mankind to be inaugurated by this amiable young king, whose kindness of heart shone forth in his first speech, "We will have no more loans, no credit, no fresh burdens on the people;" then, leaving his ministers to devise ways of paying the enormous sala-ries of officials out of an empty treasury, and to arrange the financial details of his benevolent scheme of government, he proceeded with his gay and brilliant young wife to Rheims, there to be crowned with a magnificence undreamed of by Louis XIV.

In the midst of these rejoicings over the new reign, and of speculative dreams of universal freedom, there was wafted across the Atlantic news of a handful of patriots arrayed against the tyranny of the British Crown. Here were the theories of the new philosophy translated into the reality of actual experience. "No taxation without representation," "No privileged class," "No government without the consent of the governed." Was this not an embodiment of their dreams? Nor did it detract from the interest in the conflict that England—England, the hated rival of France—was defied by an indignant people of her own race. There was not a young noble in the land who would not have rushed, if he could, to the defence of the outraged colonies.

The king, half doubting, and vaguely fearing, was swept into the current, and the armies and the courage of the Americans were splendidly reinforced by generous, enthusiastic France.

Why should the simple-hearted Louis see what no one else seemed to see: that victory or failure was alike full of peril for France? If the colonies were conquered, France would feel the hostility of England; if they were freed and self-governing, the principle of monarchy had a staggering blow.

In the mean time, as the American Revolution moved on toward success, there was talk in the cabin as well as the chateau of the "rights of man." In shops and barns, as well as in clubs and drawing-rooms, there was a glimmering of the coming day.

"What is true upon one continent is true upon another," say they. "If it is cowardly to submit to tyranny in America, what is it in France?" "If Englishmen may revolt against oppression, why may not Frenchmen?" "No government without the consent of the governed?—When has our consent been asked, the consent of twenty-five million people? Are we sheep, that we have let a few thousands govern us for a thousand years, *without* our consent?"

Poverty and hunger gave force and urgency to these questions. The people began to clamor more boldly for the good time which had been promised by the kind-hearted king. The murmur swelled to an ominous roar. Thousands were at his very palace gates, telling him in no unmistakable terms that they were tired of smooth words and fair promises. What they wanted was a new constitution and—bread.

Poor Louis! the one could be made with pen and paper; but by what miracle could he produce the other? How gladly would he have given them anything. But what could he do? There was not enough money to pay the salaries of his officials, nor for his gay young queen's fetes and balls! The old way would have been to impose new taxes. But how could he tax a people crying at his gates for bread? He made more promises which he could not keep; yielded, one after another, concessions of authority and dignity; then vacillated, and tried to return over the slippery path, only to be dragged on again by an irresistible fate.

Louis' Minister of Finance, Turgot, was a trained economist and a man of very great ability. When Louis assured the people, in the speech after his coronation, that there were to be "no more loans, no fresh burdens on the people," he did not know how Turgot was going to accomplish this miracle. He was unaware that it was to be done by cutting off the cherished privileges of the nobility, and that the proposed reforms were all aimed at the privileged classes. When this became apparent, indignation was great at Versailles. The court would not hear of economy. Turgot was dismissed, and Necker, a Swiss banker (father of Madame de Staël), called to fill his place.

Necker made another mistake. He took the people into his confidence, let them know the sources of revenue, the nature of expenditures, and measures of relief. This was very quieting to the public, but exasperating to the privileged classes, who had never taken the people into their confidence, and considered it an impertinence for them to inquire how the moneys were spent. And so Louis, again yielding to the pressure at Versailles, dismissed Necker; then, in the outburst of rage which followed, tried to retrace his steps and recall him.

But events were moving too swiftly for that now. In the existing temper of the people, small reforms and concessions were unavailing. They were demanding that the States General be called.

The critical moment had come. If Louis of his own initiative had summoned that body to confer over the situation, it would have been a very different thing; but a call of the States-General at the ***demand of the people*** was a virtual surrender of the very principle of absolutism. The work of Richelieu, Mazarin, and Louis XIV. would be undone; for it would involve an acknowledgment of the right of the people to dictate to the king, and to participate in the government of the nation. The whole revolutionary contention was vindicated in this act.

The call was issued; and when Louis, in 1789, convoked the States General, he made his last concession to the demands of his subjects.

That almost-forgotten body had not been seen since Richelieu effaced all the auxiliary functions of government. Nobles, ecclesiastics, and Tiers État (or commons) found themselves face to face once more. The courtly contemptuous nobles, the princely ecclesiastics were unchanged, but there was a new expression in the pale faces of the commons. There was a look of calm defiance as they met the disdainful gaze of the aristocrats across the gulf of two centuries.

The two superior bodies absolutely refused to sit in the same room with the commons. They might under the same roof, but in the same room—never.

There was an historic precedent for this refusal. The three estates had always acted as three separate bodies. So the demand in itself was an encroachment upon the ancient dignity of the two superior bodies, which they resented. But they might better have yielded. The Tiers État with dignity and firmness insisted that they should meet and vote together as one body, or they would constitute themselves a separate body, and act independently of the other two. This was the Rubicon. On one side compromise, and possible co-operation of the three legislative bodies; on the other, revolution, in charge of the people.

Aristocratic France was offered its last chance, and committed its last act of arrogance and folly. The ultimatum was refused by the nobles and clergy. And the Tiers État declared itself the National Assembly, in which was vested all the legislative authority of the kingdom. The people had taken possession of the Government of France!

The predetermined destruction of the monarchy seems evident, when at the most critical point, and at the moment calling for the most careful retrenchment and reform, fate had placed Louis XV., acting like a madman in the excesses of his profligacy; and, at the next stage, while the last opportunity still existed by main force to drag the nation back, and hold it from going over the brink, there stood the most excellent, the kindest-hearted but weakest gentleman who ever wore the name of king! When the distracted Louis gave the impotent order for the National Assembly to disperse, and for the three bodies to assemble and vote separately, according to ancient custom; and then when he gave still further proof of childish incompetency by telling the Tiers État they were "not to meddle with the privileges of the higher orders," kingship had become a mockery. It was a child telling the tornado not to come in that direction.

When the king's herald read to the National Assembly this foolish message, ending with the formula, "You hear, gentlemen, the orders of the king," Mirabeau sprang to his feet, saying, "Go, tell your master we are here by the will of the people, and will be only removed at the point of the bayonet," the pitiful king then yielding to this defiance, even begging the nobles and deputies of the clergy to join the National Assembly—a revolutionary assembly, which was holding its meetings in his own Palace of Versailles, and which was every day gravitating from its original lofty purpose; its rallying cry for justice and reform of abuses changing to "Down with the Aristocrats!" It was becoming alarming, so Louis ordered the body to disperse; and when soldiers stood at the door to prevent its assembling, it took possession of the queen's tennis court, and there each member took a solemn oath not to dissolve until the object they sought had been secured.

There were some among the clergy and the nobles who realized the necessity for reforms, and who would gladly have joined a movement inaugurated in a different spirit. Hence, partly from alarm, and partly impelled by other reasons and purposes, more or less pure, there was finally a secession from the two aristocratic bodies; the Duke of Orleans, cousin of the king, leading the movement in one, and three archbishops in the other. These, with their followers, appeared among the Tiers État as converts to the popular cause, the Marquis de Lafayette, hero of the late American War, sitting next to Mirabeau, the powerful and eloquent leader of the whole movement in its first days.

Concerning the genius of Mirabeau there is no difference of opinion. All are agreed that intellectually he towered far above every one about him. But whether he was the incarnation of good or of evil, the world is still in doubt; and also whether he could have guided the forces he had invoked, if a premature death had not swept him off from the scene, leaving Robespierre, a man concerning whom there is no disagreement of opinion, to guide the storm.

Paris was becoming wild with excitement. Clubs and associations were in every quarter, and detachments of a Parisian mob marched and sang at night, firing the hearts of the rabble. But it was the Palais Royal, the home of the Duke of Orleans, that friend of the people, which was the heart of the whole movement. There, patriots and lovers of France, their hearts aflame with noble aspiration for their country, met with schemers without heart, more or less wicked, the Camille Desmoulins and the Marats all fused into one body under the leadership of the Duke of Orleans, cousin of the king, who, rising superior to aristocratic traditions, believed in ***Equality,*** and was the man of the people—Philippe Egalité! His young son Louis Philippe perhaps listened with wonder to the sounds of strange revelry and the wild shouts which greeted the eloquence of Camille Desmoulins and of Marat.

At last a rumor reached the Palais Royal, and from there ran through the streets like an electric current, that the king's soldiers were marching upon the Assembly to disperse it. Mad with wine and excitement, a common impulse seized the entire populace, to destroy the Bastille, that old stronghold of despotism, that symbol of royal tyranny. This prison-fortress, with its eight great round towers, and moat eighty-three feet wide, had stood since 1371, and represented more tragic human experiences than any structure in France. In an hour the doors were burst open, and before the sun went down the heads of the governor and his officials were being carried on pikes through the streets of Paris. The horrible drama had opened. The tiger in the slums had tasted blood, and would want it again.

Thus far it was only an insurgent mob, committing violence, and the National Assembly at once created a body of militia, under the direction of Lafayette, for the protection of Paris.

When the news of the fall of the Bastille reached Versailles, the king, still failing to realize the gravity of the situation, exclaimed, "Then it is a revolt!" "Sire," said the Duke de Liancourt, "it is a Revolution!"

The king found himself deserted. His terrified nobles almost in a body were fleeing from the kingdom. Bewildered, not knowing what to do, or what not to do, and desiring to assure the people that he was their friend, he appeared before the National Assembly and made the last sacrifice—accepted the Tricolor; adopted the livery of the revolutionary party! The act was received with immense enthusiasm, and the outlook became more reassuring.

Then the garrison at the palace was re-enforced by a regiment from the country, and a dinner was given to welcome the new officers. The king and queen were urged to enter the room for a few moments, simply as an act of courtesy. Marie Antoinette most reluctantly consented to pass through the banqueting-hall. The officers, when they saw the beautiful daughter of Maria Theresa, sprang to their feet, and, flushed with wine, and in a transport of enthusiasm, committed a fatal act. Throwing their tricolors under the table, they drank to the toast, *"The king forever!"*

When this was reported in Paris the storm burst anew. A thousand terrible women, led by one still more terrible than the rest, started for Versailles. This crowd of base and degraded beings, re-enforced on the way by all that is worst, arrived at the palace, and the howling mob encamped outside in the rain all night. Entrance at last was found by someone, and they were inside and at the queen's door; she barely escaping by a hidden passageway leading to the king's room.

"The king to Paris!" was the cry; and in the morning the wretched Louis appeared upon the balcony and indicated his willingness to go to Paris as they desired. And then the queen, hoping to touch their hearts, also appeared upon the balcony, holding in her arms the dauphin, with the tricolor on his breast. And with this horrible escort they did go back to Paris, leaving Versailles forever, and were virtually prisoners at the Tuileries.

The position of Lafayette at this time is a singular one: an agent of the National Assembly, protecting the king from the Jacobins, and saying to Robespierre and Marat, "If you kill the king to-day, I will place the dauphin on the throne to-morrow."

But the currents of a cataract nearing the fall are difficult to guide. Three parties were forming in the National Assembly: the *Girondists,* the party of genius and eloquence and of moderation; the *Jacobins,* the party of the extremists and radicals; and a third party, undecided, waiting to see what was safest and best.

All that was noble and true and fine in the French Revolution was in the party of the Girondists. Dreamers, idealists, their dream was of a republic like the one in America, and their ideal an impossible perfection of condition in which human reason was supreme. The excesses of the Revolution they did not approve, but were willing to sacrifice the king and even the royal family, if necessary. They did not realize the forces with which they were airily playing, nor that the time was at hand when the Girondists would vainly strive to restrain the horrible excesses; that, after they had sacrificed the royal family, the Jacobins would sacrifice them; the slayers would be slain!

Lafayette, neither a Girondist nor a Jacobin, was a loyal Frenchman and patriot, with the American ideal in his heart, vainly trying to mediate between a feeble king and a people who had lost their reason. The time was near when he would give up the hopeless task and flee to escape being himself engulfed.

A wretchedly planned attempt at the escape of the royal family aggravated the situation. They were recognized at Varennes, brought back with great indignity, and placed under closer surveillance than before. On the 10th of August, 1792, the mob attacked the Tuileries. The royal family fled to the National Assembly for protection, while their Swiss guards vainly defended the palace with their lives.

This was the end of the monarchy. Louis, the brave queen and her children, and Princess Elizabeth, sister of the king, were removed from the Assembly to the prison in "The Temple," and the National Convention formally declared France a republic.

The grim prison to which they were taken, with its central square tower flanked by four round towers, had stood since the time of Philip Augustus. It was built for the Knights Templar, and was chateau, fortress, prison, all in one, and was the home of the grand master and those others who were burned when Philip IV. ruthlessly destroyed the order. The central tower, one hundred and fifty feet high, had four stories. The king and the dauphin were imprisoned in the second story, and the queen, her young daughter, and the Princess Elizabeth in the story above.

The power swiftly passed from Girondists to Jacobins, and a Revolutionary Tribunal was created in charge of the terrible triumvirate—Robespierre, Marat, and Danton.

An awful travesty upon a court of justice was established in that historic hall in the Palais de Justice. Its walls, which had looked down upon generations of Merovingian, Carlovingian, and Capetian kings, now beheld the condemnation of the most innocent and well-intentioned of all the kings of France.

The king was arraigned at this court upon the charge of treason, convicted, and condemned to die on the 21st of January, 1793. He was allowed to embrace for the last time his adored wife and children. At the scaffold he tried to speak a last word to his people. The drums were ordered to drown his voice, and an attendant priest uttered the words, *"Fils de Saint Louis, montez au ciel!"*—Son of Saint Louis, ascend to heaven!—and all was over. The kindest-hearted, most inoffensive gentleman in Europe had expiated the crimes of his ancestors.

More and more furious swept the torrent, gathering to itself all that was vile and outcast. Where were the pale-faced, determined patriots who sat in the National Assembly? Some of them riding with dukes and marquises to the guillotine. Was this the equality they expected when they cried, "Down with the Aristocrats"?

Did they think they could guide the whirlwind after raising it? As well whisper to the cyclone to level only the tall trees, or to the conflagration to burn only the temples and palaces.

With restraining agencies removed, religion, government, king, all swept away, that hideous brood born of vice, poverty, hatred, and despair came out from dark hiding-places; and what had commenced as a patriotic revolt had become a wild orgy of bloodthirsty demons, led by three master-demons, Robespierre, Marat, and Danton, vying with each other in ferocity. Then we see that simple girl thinking by one supreme act of heroism and sacrifice, like Joan of Arc, to save her country. Foolish child! Did she think to slay the monster devouring Paris by cutting off one of his heads? The death of Marat only added to the fury of the tempest; and the falling of Charlotte Corday's head was not more noticed than the falling of a leaf in the forest.

The slaughter of the people had been reduced to an admirable system. The public prosecutor, Fouquier-Tinville, went every day to the "Committee of Public Safety" to procure the list of the proscribed, who were immediately placed in the Conciergerie to await trial. This list was then submitted to Robespierre, who with his pencil marked the names of those who would be executed on the morrow.

The mockery of the trial of Charlotte Corday was not delayed. This girl belonged to a family of the smaller nobility. In her secluded life in the country, a mind of superior quality had fed upon the new philosophy of the period. An enthusiasm for liberty, and a horror of tyranny, had taken possession of her. In passionate sympathy with the early purposes of the Revolution, Marat seemed to her a monster, the incarnation of the spirit which would defeat the cause of Liberty. It was believed that his list of the proscribed was not confined to Paris, but that the names of thousands of victims all over France were already designated. In that extraordinary scene at her trial, when questioned, she impatiently said, "Yes, yes, I killed him. I killed one man to save a hundred thousand!"

Nothing was lacking to make this, with one exception, the most dramatic incident of the Revolution. Her eloquent address to the French people, found pinned to the waist of her dress after her execution, and her splendid courage to the end, rounds out the picturesque story of her useless martyrdom. A Girondist waiting in the Conciergerie, when he heard of her crime and end, exclaimed: "It will kill us! But she has taught us how to die!"

The end did not come so swiftly for the queen, who, after being removed from the Temple, spent seventy-two days and nights in the dark cell in that abode of horrors, the Conciergerie. Then came the trial, the inquisitorial trial, lasting all through the night in the gloom of that dimly lighted hall. And at half-past four in the morning she heard without a tremor the terrible words, "Marie Antoinette, widow of Louis Capet, the Tribunal condemns you to die." Not for a moment did this intrepid woman quail; and a small detail brings before us vividly her wonderful calmness. As she reached the stairs in her pitiful return to her cell, she said simply to the lieutenant of the gendarmes, who was at her side, "Monsieur, I can scarcely see (*Je vols d peine*); will you lead me?"

In another half hour the drums were beating in every quarter in preparation for the event; and at ten o'clock she started upon her last ride. And how bravely she met her awful fate! We forget her follies, her reckless extravagances, in admiration for her courage as she rides to her death, with hands tied behind her, sitting in that hideous tumbril, head erect, pale, proud, defiant, as if upon a throne (October 16, 1793).

The search-light of scrutiny has been turned upon this unfortunate woman for more than a century, and all that has been discovered is that she was pleasure-loving, indiscreet, and absolutely ignorant of the gravity of her responsibility in the position she occupied.

In the days of her power and splendor she lived as the average woman of her period would have done under the same circumstances—not better, and not worse. But when the time came to try her soul and test her mettle, she evinced a strength and dignity and composure surpassing belief.

If there had been any evidence of the truth of the story of the diamond neck-lace—a story which no doubt hastened the revolutionary crisis—it would certainly have been used at her trial; but it was not. It will be remembered that this necklace was one of the fatal legacies from the reign of Louis XV., who had ordered for du

Barry this gift which was to cost a sum large enough for a king's ransom. The king died before it was completed, and the story became current that Marie Antoinette, the hated Austrian woman who was ruining France by her extravagance, was negotiating for the purchase of this necklace while the people were starving!

A network of villainy is woven about the whole incident, in which the names of a cardinal and ladies high in rank are involved. The mystery may never be uncovered, but every effort to connect the queen's name with this historic scandal has failed.

Probably of all the cruelties inflicted upon this unhappy woman, none caused her such anguish as the testimony of her son before the Revolutionary Tribunal, that he had heard his mother say she "hated the French people." Placed under the care of the brutal Simon after his father's removal from the Temple, the child had become a physical and mental wreck. The queen, in her last letter to her sister the Princess Elizabeth, makes pitiful allusion to the incident, begging her to remember what he must have suffered before he said this; also reminding her how children may be taught to utter words they do not comprehend. His lesson, no doubt, had been learned by cruel tortures; and, rendered half imbecile, it was recited when the time came. None but his keeper was ever permitted to see the boy. His condition, final illness, and death are shrouded in mystery. In June, 1794, eight months after his mother's execution, it was announced that he was dead. It would be difficult to prove this event before a court of justice. There were no witnesses whose testimony would have any weight. No one was permitted to see the child who was put into that obscure grave; and many circumstances give rise to a suspicion that the boy, who might have been a source of political embarrassment in the rehabilitation of France, was disposed of in another way—dropped into an obscurity which would serve as well as death.

There was a surfeit of killing, and a waning Revolution. We are far from saying that such a thing happened. But ambitious royalists might have thought their money well expended in removing the son of the murdered king from the scene. The claim of the American dauphin, Eleazer Williams, may have been fanciful, or even false; but what safer and more effectual plan could be devised than to drop the half-imbecile heir to a throne into the heart of a tribe of Indians in an American wilderness?

When Louis XVIII. occupied his brother's throne, in 1814, and erected over the dishonored graves of his family that beautiful Chapelle Expiatoire, he also gave orders for masses to be said for the repose of the souls of his murdered kindred, whom he designated by name: Louis XVI., king; Marie Antoinette, queen, and the Princess Elizabeth, his sister. If it is true, as has been said, that the name of the dauphin was not included in this list, it is a most suggestive omission. Technically, this boy was king from the moment of his father's death until his own, and on the lists of sovereigns is called Louis XVII. Then why was there no mention of him as one of that martyred group?

Twenty-two of the Girondists who had helped to dethrone the king on that 10th of August, and later consented to his death, were now facing the same doom to which they had sent him only six months before, and by a strange fatality were under the same roof with the queen. Only a few feet, and two thin partitions, separated them; and in her cell she must have heard their impassioned voices during that dramatic banquet, the last night of their lives. And the next day this group of extraordinary men—men singularly gifted and fascinating—were all lying in one tomb, at the side of Louis XVI.

Philip Égalité, the Duke of Orleans, was to meet his Nemesis also. Brought a prisoner to that grim resting-place, he occupied the adjoining cell to that which had been the queen's, and, it is said, had assigned to him the wretched cot she no longer needed. His desperate game had failed. No elevation would come to him out of the chaos of crime, and the reward for scheming and voting for the death of his cousin, the king, would be a scaffold, not a throne. His name had been upon the list of the proscribed for some time; but the end was precipitated by an act of his young son, Louis Philippe, then Duke de Chartres, and aide-de-camp to Dumouriez, who was defending the frontier from an invasion of Austrian troops. After the execution of the queen, Dumouriez refused longer to defend France from an invasion the purpose of which was to make such horrors impossible. He laid down his command, and, with his aide, Louis Philippe, joined the colony of exiles in Belgium, while the Austrian troops were in full march upon Paris from Verdun.

This was treason—whether justifiable or not this is not the place to discuss.

Philip Égalité knew that he no longer had the confidence of the leaders, and that they also knew that he was an aristocrat in disguise. So when this defection of

Dumouriez came, and was shared by his own son, he tried to get out of the country. He was arrested at Marseilles, brought to the Conciergerie, that halfway house to the scaffold, and was soon following in the footsteps of his king and queen, through the Rue St. Honoré, passing his own Palais Royal on his way to the Place de la Revolution.

The Revolution, beginning with a patriotic assembly, in a measure sane, had made a rapid descent, first falling apart into Girondist and Jacobin, moderate and extremist, the Girondist with a shudder consenting to the execution of the king. Then, the power passing to a so-called "Committee of Public Safety" and a Triumvirate, in order to sweep away the obstructive Girondist; and then an untrammelled Terror, in the hands of three, and, finally, one. Such had been its mad course. But with the death of the king and queen the madness had reached its height, and a revulsion of feeling set in. There was a surfeit of blood, and an awakening sense of horror, which turned upon the instigators. Danton fell, and finally, when amid cries of "Death to the tyrant!" Robespierre was dragged wounded and shivering to the fate he had brought upon so many thousands, the drama which had opened at the Bastille was fittingly closed.

The great battle for human liberty had been fought and won. Religious freedom and political freedom were identical in principle. The right of the human conscience, proclaimed by Luther in 1517, had in 1793 only expanded into the large conception of all the inherent rights of the ***individual.***

It had taken centuries for English persistence to accomplish what France, with such appalling violence, had done in as many years. It had been a furious outburst of pent-up force; but the work had been thorough. Not a germ of tyranny remained. The incrustations of a thousand years were not alone broken, but pulverized; the privileged classes were swept away, and their vast estates, two-thirds of the territory of France, ready to be distributed among the rightful owners of the soil, those who by toil and industry could win them. France was as new as if she had no history. There was ample opportunity for her people now. What would they do with it?

What would they build upon the ruins of their ancient despotism? What would be the starting-point for such a task—every connecting link with an historic past broken, and the armies of an indignant Europe pressing in upon every side? Could they ever wipe out the stain which had made them odious in the sight of Christendom? Would they ever be forgiven for disgracing the name of Liberty?

It was the power and genius of a single man which was going to make the world forget her disgrace, and cover France with a mantle more glorious than she had ever worn.

CHAPTER XVI.

The Revolution over, France, sitting among the wreckage of the past, found herself disgraced, discredited, and at war with all of Europe. Austria, naturally the leader in an effort to stop the atrocities which threatened a daughter of her own royal house, had been joined finally by England, Holland, Spain, and even Portugal and Tuscany, these all being impelled, not by the personal feeling which actuated Austria, but by alarm for their own safety. This revolutionary movement was a moral and political plague spot which must be stamped out, or there would be anarchy in every kingdom in Europe.

It was the difficulty in recruiting troops to fight this coalition which had embarrassed and finally broken the power of the revolutionary government. If the states of Europe had really acted in concert, the life of the new republic would have been brief. But Austria was jealous of Prussia, and Prussia afraid of the friendship which was forming between Austria and England, and Catharine, the empress of Russia, keeping all uncertain about her designs upon Poland—with the result that the war upon France was conducted in a desultory and ineffectual manner.

In the organization of the new French republic, the executive power was vested in a ***Directory,*** composed of five members, chosen by two houses of legislature.

A disagreement over some details of the new constitution led to a heated quarrel, and this to an insurrection in Paris, October 5, 1795, which Napoleon Bonaparte, a young officer who had acquired distinction at Toulon, was summoned to quell. The vigor and the success with which the young leader used his cannon in the streets of Paris struck precisely the right note at the right moment. Law and order were established. A delighted Directory yielded at once to the suggestion of a campaign against Austria which should be conducted in Italy, in combination with an advance upon Vienna from the Rhine.

With the instinct of genius, Napoleon Bonaparte saw the path to power. The air was vibrating with the word **Liberty.** If he would capture France—which was what he intended to do—he must move along the line of political freedom. The note to be struck was the liberation of the oppressed. Where would he find chains more galling, more unnatural, than in Italy, held by the iron hand of Austria? And was not Austria the leader of the coalition against France?

Without money or supplies, and with an unclothed army, he obeyed the inspiration, audaciously planning to make the invaded country pay the expenses of the war waged against it. Pointing to the Italian cities, he said to his soldiers: "There is your reward. It is rich and ample, but you must conquer it!" Like Caesar, he knew how, in words brief and concise, to address his followers, and to inspire enthusiasm as few have ever done before or since. He also knew how to confound the enemy with new and unexpected methods which made unavailing all which military science and experience had taught them.

With the suddenness of a tornado he swept down upon the plains of Lombardy. The battles of **Lodi, Arcola, Rivoli,** were won, and in ten months Napoleon was master of Italy. By the treaty of Campo Formio, October 17, 1797, northern Italy was divided into four republics, with their capitals respectively at Milan, Genoa, Bologna, and Rome. And in return for her acquiescence in this redistribution of her Italian territory, Austria received Venice. After fourteen centuries of independence, Venetia, the queen of the Adriatic, was in chains!

Not satisfied with this, Napoleon intended that Paris should wear the jewels which had adorned the fair Italian cities. The people whose chains he had come to break were, at once required to surrender money, jewels, plate, horses, equipments, besides their choicest art collections and rarest manuscripts. In a private letter to a member of the Directory he wrote: "I shall send you twenty pictures by some of the first masters, including Correggio and Michael Angelo." A later letter said: "Join all these to what will be sent from Rome and we shall have all that is beautiful in Italy, except a small number of objects in Turin and Naples." Pius VI., without a protest, surrendered his millions of francs, and ancient bronzes, costly pictures, and priceless manuscripts.

Austria had lost fourteen battles, and all her Italian possessions were grouped together into a Cisalpine republic! Another Helvetic republic was set up in Switzerland, and still another republic created in Holland under a French protectorate.

In other words, this man had accomplished in Italy precisely what he was going to accomplish later in Germany. He had broken down the lingering traces of medievalism, and prepared the soil for a new order of things.

The peace of Campo Formio was the most glorious ever made for France. The river Rhine was at last recognized as her frontier, thus placing Belgium within the lines of the republic. Napoleon had captured not alone Italy, but France herself? What might she not accomplish with such a leader? The delighted Directory discussed the invasion of England. Napoleon, knowing this would be premature, dramatically conceived the idea of crippling England by threatening her Asiatic possessions, and led an army into Egypt (1798). Although Nelson destroyed his fleet, he still maintained the arrogance of a conqueror.

No king, no military leader, had brought as much glory to France. Du Guesclin, Turenne, Condé, all were eclipsed. And so were Marlborough and Prince Eugene. What would not France do at the bidding of this magician, who by a single sweep of his wand had raised her from the dust of humiliation and made her the leading power on the Continent!

The young officer, now so distinguished, had married in the early part of his career the widow of M. de Beauharnais, one of the victims of the Reign of Terror. During his absence in Egypt, the Directorate, and the Legislature, and the people had all become embroiled in dissensions. Things were falling again into chaos, with no hand to hold them together. Discontent was rife, and men were asking why the one man, the little dark man who knew how to do and to compel things, and to maintain discipline, why he was sent to the Nile and the Pyramids!

Josephine, from Paris, kept Napoleon informed of these conditions. So, leaving his army in charge of Kléber, he unexpectedly returned. He knew what he was going to do; and he also knew he could depend upon the army to sustain him. By political moves as adroit and unexpected as his tactics on the field, the Directorate was swept out of existence, and Napoleon was first consul of France.

It was a long step backward. The pendulum was returning once more toward a strong executive, and to centralization. From this moment, until he was a prisoner in the hands of the English, Napoleon Bonaparte was sole master of France.

The early simplicity of the republic was disappearing. The receptions of the first consul at the Tuileries began to recall the days at Versailles. Josephine, fascinating, and perfect in the art of dress, knew well how to maintain the splendor of her new court; as also did Bonaparte's sisters, with their beauty and their brilliant talents. But outside of France, and across the channel, the consul was only a usurper, and Louis XVIII. was king—an uncrowned but legitimate sovereign!

Perhaps it is not too much to say that nothing in Napoleon's career has left such enduring traces, and so permanently influenced civilization, as two acts performed at this period: the creation of that monumental work of genius the codification of the laws of France and the sale of Louisiana to the United States. Spain had ceded this large territory to France in 1763, and Bonaparte realizing that he was not in a position to hold it now, if attacked, sold it to the United States (1803), in order to keep it out of the hands of England.

The goal to which things were tending was realized by some. A conspiracy against the life of the consul was discovered. Napoleon suspected it to have originated with the Bourbons; and the death of the young Duke d'Enghien, a son of the Prince of Condé, without pity or justice, was intended to strike with terror all who were plotting for his downfall. The swiftness with which it was done, the darkness under the walls of Vincennes, the lantern on the breast of the victim, and the file of soldiers at midnight, all conspired to warn conspirators of the fate awaiting them. It was the critical moment at hand which turned Bonaparte's heart to steel.

Only a few days after this tragedy at Vincennes a proposition was made in the Tribunate to bestow upon the first consul the title of hereditary Emperor of the French!

This new Charlemagne did not go to the pope to be crowned, as that other had done in the year 800; but at his bidding the pope came to him. And when on the 2d of December, 1804, the crown of France was placed upon his head, the great drama commenced in 1789 had ended. Rivers of blood had flowed to free her from despotism, and France was held by a power more despotic than that of Richelieu or of Louis XIV.

At war with all of Europe, Napoleon swiftly unfolded his great plan not only to conquer, but to demolish—not one state, but all. He was going to create an empire out of a federation of European kingdoms all held in his own hand, and to tear in pieces the old map of Europe, precisely as he had the map of Italy. He was going to break down the old historic divisions and landmarks, and create new, as he had created a kingdom of Italy out of Italian republics. So, while he was fighting a combined Europe, Bavaria, Würtemberg, and Saxony had become kingdoms, and the West German States, seventeen in number, were all merged in a Confederation of the Rhine, "the Rheinbund," under a French Protectorate.

Then Austria felt the weight of his hand. Francis Joseph wore the double crown created by Charlemagne a thousand years before, and was Emperor of Rome as well as of Germany. It had become an empty title; but it was the sacred tradition of a Holy Roman Empire, the empire which had dominated the world during the Middle Ages, and while Europe was coming into form. Napoleon was ploughing deep into the soil of the past when he told Francis Joseph he must drop the title of Emperor of Rome! And it is a startling indication of his power that the emperor unresistingly obeyed; the logical meaning, of course, being that he, already King of Italy, was the successor to Charlemagne and the head of a new Roman Empire.

England, never having felt the touch of this insolent conqueror upon her own soil, was still the bitterest of all in the coalition, and was more indignant over the humiliation of Germany than she seemed to be herself. Prussia, at last reluctantly opposing him, was defeated at Jena, 1806, a time during which the beautiful Queen Louise was the heroine, and the one brave enough to defy him; and then the peace of Tilsit, 1807, completed the humiliation of the kingdom created by the great elector.

It would seem that the people as well as the armies of Germany were captured by this man, when we hear that ninety German authors dedicated their books to him, a servile press praised him, and one of Beethoven's greatest sonatas was inspired by him. But a man so colossal and dazzling could only be accurately measured at a distance. Even yet we are too near to him for that, and the world has not yet come to an agreement concerning him, any more than as to the true analysis of the character of Hamlet.

There was now scarcely an uncrowned head in Napoleon's family. His brother Louis, who had married his step-daughter, Hortense Beauharnais, was king of Holland. His brother-in-law Murat he made king of Naples; Eugene Beauharnais, his step-son, viceroy of Italy; his brother Jerome, King of Westphalia; and then his brother Joseph was placed upon the throne of Spain, from which an indignant people drove him ingloriously away.

In an hour's interview with Alexander, Emperor of Russia, Napoleon had by the magic of superiority secured that emperor's friendship and co-operation in his plans against England. All this excellent man was fighting for was the peace of Europe! And he disclosed to Alexander his plan that they two should be the eternal custodians of that peace; which was to be secured by restraining the arrogance of England, and that was to be done by ruining the commercial prosperity of that nation of shopkeepers. There was to be organized a continental blockade against England. Europe was to be forbidden to trade with that country.

A plan was forming in the mind of Napoleon which was destined as the turning-point in his astonishing career. It was of vast importance to him that he should have an heir to the great inheritance he was creating. By repudiating Josephine, and marrying the daughter of Francis Joseph, there might be an heir who would also be the legitimate descendant of the Cæsars; thus immensely fortifying the empire after his own death.

When this thought took possession of his mind, the psychological moment had arrived. The tide had turned toward disaster. The marriage with Maria Louisa took place at Paris in 1810. The marriage of Napoleon with a Hapsburg was not pleasing to the French people, who took pride in the simple origin of their emperor and empress. This hero of Marengo, and Austerlitz, and Jena, and Wagram, the man before whom Europe trembled, was he not, after all, only a crowned citizen? And was this not a triumph for the revolutionary principle which offset the existence of an empire, as its final result?

Alexander had broken away from his agreement and his friendship with the emperor, and had joined the allies. So in 1812 the long-contemplated invasion of Russia began. Of the 678,000 souls recruited chiefly from conquered states, only 80,000 would ever return. Never before had Napoleon fought the elements, and never before met overwhelming defeat! The flames at Moscow, followed by the arctic cold, converted the campaign into a vast tragedy.

With indomitable courage another grand army had filled the vacant places, and was putting down a great uprising in Germany. But his star was waning. An overwhelming defeat at Leipsic was followed by a march upon Paris. And in the spring of 1814, Alexander, the young Russian emperor, the friend who was to aid him in securing an eternal peace for Europe, was dictating the terms of surrender in Paris.

Within a week Napoleon had abdicated. The title of emperor he was permitted to retain, but the empire which he was to leave to the infant son of Maria Louisa, now two years old, had shrunk to the little island of Elba, on the west coast of Italy!

CHAPTER XVII.

THE allied powers named Louis XVIII., the brother of Louis XVI., for the vacant throne, who promised the people to reign under a constitutional government.

The man who had deserted his brother in his extremity, a man who represented nothing—not loyalty to the past, nor sympathy with a single aspiration of the present—was king. As he passed under triumphal arches on the way to the Tuileries, there was sitting beside him a sad, pale-faced woman; this was the Duchesse d'Angoulême, the daughter of Louis XVI., the little girl who was prisoner in the Temple twenty years before. What must she have felt and thought as she passed the very spot where had stood the scaffold in 1793!

Almost the first act of Louis XVIII. was the removal of the mutilated remains of the king and queen and his sister Elizabeth to the royal vault in the Church of St. Denis. He then gave orders for a ***Chapelle Expiatoire*** to be erected over the grave where they had been lying for two decades, and for masses to be said for the repose of the souls of his murdered relatives. Paris was full of returning royalists. Banished exiles with grand old names, who had been earning a scanty living by teaching French and dancing in Vienna, London, and even in New York, were hastening to Paris for a joyful Restoration; and Louis XVIII., while Russian and Austrian troops guarded him on the streets of his own capital, was freely talking about ruling by divine right!

That king was reigning under a liberal charter (as the new constitution was called)—a charter which guaranteed almost as much personal liberty as the one obtained in England from King John in 1215; and the palpable absurdity of supposing that he and his supporters might at the same time revive and maintain Bourbon traditions, as if there had been no Revolution, was at least not an indication of much sagacity.

But there was a very smooth surface. The tricolor had disappeared. Napoleon's generals had gone unresistingly over to the Bourbons. Talleyrand adapted himself as quickly to the new régime as he had to the Napoleonic; was witty at the expense of the empire and the emperor, who, as he said, "was not even a Frenchman"; and was as crafty and as useful an instrument for the new ruler as he had been for the pre-existing one.

But something was happening under the surface. While the plenipotentiaries were busy over their task of restoring boundaries in Europe, and the other restoration was going on pleasantly in Paris, a rumor came that Napoleon was in Lyons. A regiment was at once despatched to drive him back; and Marshal Ney, "the bravest of the brave," was sent with orders to arrest him.

The next news that came to Paris was that the troops were frantically shouting *"Vive l'empereur!"* and Ney was embracing his beloved commander and pledging his sword in his service.

At midnight the king left the Tuileries for the Flemish frontier, and before the dawn Napoleon was in his Palace of Fontainebleau (March 20th), which he had left exactly eleven months before. The night after the departure of the king there suddenly appeared lights passing swiftly over the Pont de la Concorde; then came the tramp of horses' feet, and a carriage attended on each side by cavalry with drawn swords. The carriage stopped at the first entrance to the garden of the Tuileries, and a small man with a dark, determined face was borne into the palace the Bourbon had just deserted.

There was consternation in the Council Chamber in London when the Duke of Wellington entered and announced that Napoleon was in Paris, and all must be done over again!

Immediate preparations were made for a renewal of the war. It was easy to find men to fight the emperor's battles. All France was at his feet.

The decisive moment was at hand. Napoleon had crossed into the Netherlands, and Wellington was waiting to meet him.

The struggle at Waterloo had lasted many hours. The result, so big with fate, was trembling in the balance, when suddenly the booming of Prussian guns was heard, and Wellington was re-enforced by Blücher. This was the end. The French were defeated (June 18, 1815). Napoleon was in the hands of the English, and was to be carried a life-prisoner to the island of St. Helena.

Louis XVIII., who had been waiting at Ghent, immediately returned to the Tuileries, and to his foolish task of posing as a liberal king to his people, and as a re-actionary one to his royalist adherents. The country was full of disappointed, imbittered imperialists, and of angry and revengeful royalists. The Chamber of Peers immediately issued a decree for the perpetual banishment of the family of Bonaparte from French soil; the extremists demanding that the families of the men who had consented to the death of Louis XVI. be included in the decree. Sentence of death was passed upon Marshal Ney, as a traitor to France. Some might have said that a greater traitor was at the Tuileries; but the most picturesque in that heroic group of Napoleon's marshals was shot to death.

There was, in fact, a determined purpose to undo all the work of the Revolution; to restore the supremacy and the property of the Church, and the power of the nobility. In the meantime, the people, perfectly aware that the returned exiles were impoverished, were paying taxes to maintain foreign troops which were in France for the sole purpose of enabling the king's government to accomplish these things!

Here was material enough for discord in a troubled reign which lasted nine years. Louis XVIII. died September 16, 1824; and the Count of Artois, the brother of two kings, was proclaimed Charles X. of France.

If there had been any doubt about the real sentiments of Louis XVIII., it must have been dispelled by the last act of his reign, when, at the bidding of the Holy Alliance, he sent French soldiers to put down the Spanish liberals in their fight for a constitution.

But Charles X. did not intend to assume the thin mask worn by his brother. He had marked out a different course. All disguise was to be thrown aside in a Bourbon reign of the ante-revolutionary sort. The press was strictly censored, the charter altered, the law of primogeniture restored; and when saluted on the streets of Paris by cries of "Give us back our charter!" the answer made to his people by this infatuated man was, "I am here to receive homage, not counsel."

One wonders that a brother of Louis XVI., one who had been a fugitive from a Paris mob in 1789—if he had a memory—dared to exasperate the people of

France.

On the 29th of July a revolt had become a Revolution, and once more the Marquis de Lafayette was in charge of the municipal troops, which assembled at St. Cloud and other defensive points.

In vain did Charles protest that he would revoke every offensive ordinance, and restore the charter. It was too late.

Louis Philippe, Duke of Orleans, was appointed lieutenant-general of the kingdom. When he appeared at the Hotel de Ville wearing the tricolor, his future was already assured.

There was only one thing left now for Charles to do: he formally abdicated, and signed the paper authorizing the appointment of his cousin to the position of lieutenant-general; and ten days later, Louis Philippe, son of Philippe Egalité, occupied the throne he left.

The note struck by this new king was the absolute surrender of the principle of divine right. He was a "citizen king"; his title being bestowed not by a divine hand, but by the people, whose voice was the voice of God! The title itself bore witness to a new order of things. Louis Philippe was not King of France, but "King of the French." King of France carried with it the old feudal idea of proprietorship and sovereignty; while a King of the French was merely a leader of the people, not the owner of their soil. The charter and all existing conditions were modified to conform to this ideal, and on the 9th of August the reign of the constitutional king began.

It was the middle class in France which supported this reign; the class below that would never forget that he was, after all, a Bourbon and a king; while the two classes above, both royalists and imperialists, were unfriendly, one regarding him as a usurper on the throne of the legitimate king, and the other as a weakling unfit to occupy the throne of Napoleon.

When Charles X. tried to secure the banishment of the families of the men who had voted for the death of Louis XVI., he may have had in mind his cousin, the son of Philippe Egalité, the wickedest and most despicable of the regicides. Whatever his father had been, Louis Philippe was far from being a wicked man. Whether teaching school in Switzerland, or giving French lessons in America, he was the kindest-hearted and most inoffensive of gentlemen. The only trouble with this reign was that it was not heroic. The most emotional and romantic people in Europe had a commonplace king. Only once was there a throb of genuine enthusiasm during the eighteen years of his occupancy of the throne, and that was when the remains of their adored Napoleon were brought from St. Helena and placed in that magnificent tomb in the Hotel des Invalides by order of the king, who sent his son, the Prince de Joinville, to bring this gift to the people. The act was gracious, but it was also hazardous. Perhaps the king did not know how slight was his hold upon this imaginative people, nor the possible effect of contrast.

Under the new order of things in a constitutional monarchy the king does not govern, he reigns. He was chosen by the people as their ornamental figure-head. But what if he ceased to be ornamental? What was the use of a king who in eighteen years had added not a single ray of glory to the national name, but who was using his high position to increase his enormous private fortune, and incessantly begging an impoverished country for benefits and emoluments for five sons?

An excellent father, truly, though a shortsighted one. His power had no roots. The cutting from the Orleans tree had never taken hold upon the soil, and toppled over at the sound of Lamartine's voice proclaiming a republic from the balcony of the Hotel de Ville.

When invited to step down from his royal throne, he did so on the instant. Never did king succumb with such alacrity, and never did retiring royalty look less imposing than when Louis Philippe was in hiding at Havre under the name of "William Smith," waiting for safe convoy to England, without having struck one blow in defence of his throne.

But three terrible words had floated into the open windows of the Tuileries. With the echoes of 1792 still sounding in his ears, "Liberty," "Equality," and "Fraternity," shouted in the streets of Paris, had not a pleasant sound!

Republicanism was an abiding sentiment in France, even while two dull Bourbon kings were stupidly trying to turn back the hands on the dial of time, and while an Orleans, with more supple neck, was posing as a popular sovereign. During all this tiresome interlude the real fact was developing. A Republican sentiment which had existed vaguely in the air was materializing, consolidating, into a more and more tangible reality in the minds of thinking men and patriots.

The ablest men in the country stood with plans matured, ready to meet this crisis. A republic was proclaimed; M. de Lamartine, Ledru-Rollin, General Cavaignac, M. Raspail, and Louis Napoleon were rival candidates for the office of President.

The nephew of Napoleon Bonaparte, and son of Hortense, was only known as the perpetrator of two very absurd attempts to overthrow the monarchy under Louis Philippe. But since the remains of the great emperor had been returned to France by England, and the splendors of the past placed in striking contrast with a dull, lustreless present, there had been a revival of Napoleonic memories and enthusiasm. Here was an opportunity to unite two powerful sentiments in one man—a Napoleon at the head of republican France would express the glory of the past and the hope of the future.

The magic of the name was irresistible. Louis Napoleon was elected President of the second Republic, and history prepared to repeat itself.

CHAPTER XVIII.

A REVOLUTION scarcely deserving the name had made France a second time a republic. The Second French Republic was the creation of no particular party. In fact, it seemed to have sprung into being spontaneously out of the soil of discontent.

Its immediate cause was the forbidding of a banquet which was arranged to take place in Paris on Washington's birthday, February 22d, 1848. M. Guizot, who had succeeded M. Thiers as head of the ministry, knowing the political purpose for which it was intended, and that it was a part of an impending demonstration in the hands of dangerous agitators, would not permit the banquet to take place.

This was the signal for an insurrection by a Paris mob, which immediately led to a change in the form of government—a crisis which the nation had taken no part in inaugurating. Revolution had been written in French history in very large Roman capitals! But when the smoke from this smallest of revolutions had curled away, there stood Louis Napoleon—son of the great Bonaparte's brother Louis and Hortense de Beauharnais—who had been elected president by vote of the nation.

France did not know whether she was pleased or not. Inexperienced in the art of government, she only knew that she wanted prosperity, and conditions which would give opportunity to the genius of her people. Any form of government, or any ruler who could produce these, would be accepted. She had suffered much, and was bewildered by fears of anarchy on one side and of tyranny on the other. If she looked doubtfully at this dark, mysterious, unmagnetic man, she remembered it was only for four years, and was as safe as any other experiment; and the author of those two ridiculous attempts at a restoration of the empire, made at Strasbourg and at Boulogne, was not a man to be feared.

The overthrow of monarchy in France had, however, been taken more seriously in other countries than at home. It had kindled anew the fires of republicanism all over Europe: Kossuth leading a revolution in Hungary, and Garibaldi and Mazzini in Italy, where Victor Emmanuel, the young King of Sardinia, was at the moment in deadly struggle with Austria over the possession of Milan, and dreaming of the day when a united Italy would be freed from the Austrian yoke.

The man at the head of the French Republic was surveying all these conditions with an intelligence, strong and even subtle, of which no one suspected him, and viewed with satisfaction the extinguishment of the revolutionary fires in Europe, which had been kindled by the one in France to which he owed his own elevation!

The Assembly soon realized that in this prince-president it had no automaton to deal with. A deep antagonism grew, and the cunningly devised issue could not fail to secure popular support to Louis Napoleon. When an assembly is at war with the president because *it* desires to restrict the suffrage, and *he* to make it universal, can anyone doubt the result? He was safe in appealing to the people on such an issue, and sure of being sustained in his proclamation dissolving the Assembly.

The Assembly refused to be dissolved. Then, on the morning of December 2, 1851, there occurred the famous coup d'état, *when all the leading members were arrested at their homes, and Louis Napoleon, relying absolutely upon their suffrages, stood before the French nation, with a constitution already prepared, which actually bestowed imperial powers upon himself. And the suddenness and the audacious spirit with which it was done really pleased a people wearied by incompetency in their rulers; and so, just one year later, in 1852, the nation ratified the* coup d'état by voluntarily offering to Louis Napoleon the title, Napoleon III., Emperor of the French.

His Mephistophelian face did not look as classic under the laurel wreath as had his uncle's, nor had his work the blinding splendor nor the fineness of texture of his great model. But then, an imitation never has. It was a marble masterpiece, done in plaster! But what a clever reproduction it was! And how, by sheer audacity, it compelled recognition and homage, and at last even adulation in Europe!—and what a clever stroke it was, for this heavy, unsympathetic man to bring up to his throne from the people a radiant empress, who would capture romantic and aesthetic France!

It was a far cry from cheap lodgings in New York to a seat upon the imperial throne of Prance; but human ambition is not easily satisfied. A Pelion always rises beyond an Ossa. It was not enough to feel that he had re-established the prosperity and prestige of France, that fresh glory had been added to the Napoleonic name. Was there not, after all, a certain irritating reserve in the homage paid him? was there not a touch of condescension in the friendship of his royal neighbors? And had he not always a Mordecai at his gate—while the ***Faubourg St. Germain*** stood aloof and disdainful, smiling at his brand-new aristocracy?

War is the thing to give solidity to empire and to reputation! So, when invited to join the allies in a war upon Russia in defence of Turkey, Louis Napoleon accepted with alacrity. France had no interests to serve in the Crimean War (1854-56); but the newly made emperor did not underestimate the value of this recognition by his royal neighbors, and French soldiers and French gun-boats largely contributed to the success of the allied forces in the East.

The little Kingdom of Sardinia, as the nucleus of the new Italy was called, had also joined the allies in this war; and thus a slender tie had been created between her and France at a time when Austria was savagely attacking her possessions in the north of Italy.

When Napoleon was privately sounded by Count Cavour, he named as his price for intervention in Italy two things: the cession to France of the Duchy of Savoy, and the marriage of his cousin, Jerome Bonaparte, with Clotilde, the young daughter of Victor Emmanuel. Savoy was the ancestral home of the king, and the only thing he loved more than Savoy was his daughter Clotilde, just fifteen years old. The terms were hard, but they were accepted.

When Louis Napoleon entered Italy with his army in 1859, it was as a liberator—dramatically declaring that he came to "give Italy to herself"; that she was to be "free, from the Alps to the Adriatic"! The victory at Magenta was the first step toward the realization of this glorious promise; quickly followed by another at Solferino. Milan was restored, Lombardy was free, and as the news sped toward the south the Austrian dukes of Tuscany, Modena, and Parma fled in dismay, and these rejoicing states offered their allegiance, not to the King of Sardinia, now, but to the King of Italy. There were only two more states to be freed, only Venetia and the papal state of Rome, and a "United Italy" would indeed be "free from the Alps to the Adriatic."

Then the unexpected happened. The dramatic pledge was not to be kept. Venetia was not to be liberated. The Peace of Villafranca was signed. Austria relinquished Lombardy, but was permitted to retain Venice. Cavour, white with rage, said, "Cut loose from the traitor! Refuse Lombardy!" But Victor Emmanuel saw more clearly the path of wisdom; and so, after only two months of warfare, Napoleon was taking back to France Savoy and Nice as trophies of his brilliant expedition.

This liberator of an Italy which was not liberated, would have liked to restore the fleeing Austrian dukes to their respective thrones in Florence, Modena, and Parma; but he did what was more effectual and pleasing to the enemies of a united Italy: he garrisoned Rome with French troops, and promised Pius IX. any needed protection for the papal throne.

One can imagine how Garibaldi's heart was wrung when he exclaimed, "That man has made me a foreigner in my own city!" And so might have said the king himself.

The emperor and the empire had been immensely strengthened by the Italian campaign. France was rejoicing in a phenomenal prosperity, reaching every part of the land. There was a new France and a new Paris; new boulevards were made, gardens and walks and drives laid out, and a renewed and magnificent city extended from the Bois de Vincennes on one side to the Bois de Boulogne on the other. With the building of public works there was occupation for all, resulting in the repose for which France had longed.

The Empress Eugénie was beautiful and gracious, and her court at Versailles, Fontainebleau, and the Tuileries compared well in splendor with the traditions of the past.

The emperor's ambitions began to take on a larger form. Under the auspices of the government, M. Lesseps commenced a transisthmian canal, which would open communication between the Mediterranean Sea and the Red Sea. Then, in 1862, a less peaceful scheme developed. An expedition was planned to Mexico, against which country France had a small grievance.

The United States was at this time fighting for its life in a civil war of gigantic proportions. The time was favorable for a plan conceived by the emperor to convert Mexico into an empire under a French protectorate. The principle known as the Monroe Doctrine forbade the establishment of any European power upon the Western hemisphere; but the United States was powerless at the moment to defend it, and by the time her hands were free, even if she were not disrupted, an Empire of Mexico would be established, and French troops could defend it.

In a few months the French army was in the city of Mexico, and an Austrian prince was proclaimed emperor of a Mexican empire.

This ill-conceived expedition came to a tragic and untimely end in 1867. The civil war ended triumphantly for the Union. Napoleon, realizing that, with her hands free, the United States would fight for the maintenance of the Monroe Doctrine, promptly withdrew the French army from Mexico, leaving the emperor to his fate. A republic was at once established, and the unfortunate Maximilian was ordered to be shot.

The finances of France and the prestige of the emperor had both suffered from this miserable attempt. At the same time, something had occurred which changed the entire European problem in a way most distasteful to Louis Napoleon. Prussia, in a seven weeks' war, had wrenched herself free from Austria (1866). Instead of a disrupted United States, which he had expected, there was a disrupted German Empire which he did not expect!

The triumph of Protestant Prussia was a triumph of liberalism. It meant a new political power, a rearrangement of the political problem in Europe, with Austria and despotism deposed. This was a distinct blow to the Emperor's policy, and to the headship in Europe which was its aim. Then, too, the Crimea, Magenta, and Solferino looked less brilliant since this transforming seven-weeks' war, behind which stood Bismarck with his wide-reaching plans.

His own magnificent scheme of a Hapsburg empire in Mexico under a French protectorate -had failed, and now there had suddenly arisen, as if out of the ground, a new political Germany which rivalled France in strength. The thing to do was to recover his waning prestige by a victory over Prussia.

The Empress Eugénie, devoutly Catholic in her sympathies, saw, in the ascendancy of Protestant Prussia and the humiliation of Catholic Austria, an impious blow aimed at the Catholic faith in Europe. So, as the emperor wanted war, and the empress wanted it, it only remained to make France want it too; for war it was to be.

Only one obstacle existed: there was nothing to fight about! But that was overcome. In 1870 the heart of the people of France was fired by the news that the French Ambassador had been publicly insulted by the kindly old King William. There had been some diplomatic friction over the proposed occupancy of a vacant throne in Spain by a member of the Hohenzollern (Prussian) family.

Whether true or false, the rumor served the desired purpose. France was in a blaze of indignation, and war was declared.

Not a shadow of doubt existed as to the result as the French army moved away bearing with it the boy prince imperial, that he might witness the triumph. Not only would the French soldiers carry everything before them, but the southern German States would welcome them as deliverers, and the new confederation would fall in pieces in their hands. The birthday of Napoleon I., August 15th, must be celebrated in Berlin!

This was the way it looked in France. How was it in Germany? There was no North and no South German. Men and states sprang together as a unit, under the command of Moltke and the Crown Prince Frederick William.

The French troops never got beyond their own frontier. In less than three weeks they were fighting for their existence on their own soil. In less than a month the French emperor was a prisoner, and in seven weeks his empire had ceased to exist.

The surrender of Metz, August 4th, and of Sedan, September 2d, were monumental disasters. With the news of the latter, and of the capture of the emperor, the Assembly immediately declared the empire at an end, and proclaimed a third republic in France.

Two hundred and fifty thousand German troops were marching on Paris. Fortifications were rapidly thrown about the city, and the siege, which was to last four months, had commenced.

The capitulation, which was inevitable from the first, took place in January, 1871. The terms of peace offered by the Germans were accepted, including the loss of Alsace and Lorraine, and an enormous war indemnity.

The Germans were in Paris, and King William, the Crown Prince (***Unser Fritz***), Bismarck, and Von Moltke were quartered at Versailles; and in that place, saturated with historic memories, there was enacted a strange and unprecedented scene. On January 18, 1871, in the Hall of Mirrors, King William of Prussia was formally proclaimed Emperor of a new German Empire. Ludwig II., that picturesque young King of Bavaria, in the name of the rest of the German states, laid their united allegiance at his feet, and begged him to accept the crown of a united Germany.

Moved by his colossal misfortunes, and perhaps partly in displeasure at having a French republic once more at her door, England offered asylum to the deposed emperor. There, from the seclusion of Chiselhurst, he and his still beautiful Eugenie watched the republic weathering the first days of storm and stress.

IMMEDIATELY after the deposition of the emperor a third Republic of France was proclaimed. A temporary government was set up under the direction of MM. Favre, Gambetta, Simon, Ferry, Rochefort, and others of pronounced republican tendencies.

This was speedily superseded by a National Assembly elected by the people, with M. Thiers acting as its executive head.

During the siege of Paris an internal enemy had appeared, more dangerous, and proving in the end far more destructive to the city than the German army which occupied it.

What is known as the Paris Commune was a mob of desperate men led by Socialistic and Anarchistic agitators of the kind which at intervals try to terrorize civilization to-day.

The ideas at the basis of this insurrection were the same as those which converted a patriotic revolution into a "Reign of Terror" in 1789, and Paris into a slaughter-house in 1792-93.

Twice during the siege had there been violent and alarming outbreaks from this vicious element; and now it was in desperate struggle with the government of

M. Thiers for control of that city, which they succeeded in obtaining. M. Thiers, his government, and his troops were established at Versailles; while Paris, for two months, was in the hands of these desperadoes, who were sending out their orders from the Hotel de Ville.

When finally routed by Marshal MacMahon's troops, after drenching some of the principal buildings with petroleum they set them on fire. The Tuileries and the Hotel de Ville were consumed, as were also portions of the Louvre, the Palais Royal, and the Palais de Luxembourg, and the city in many places defaced and devastated.

The insurrection was not subdued without a savage conflict, ten thousand insurgents, it is said, being killed during the last week; this being followed by severe military executions. Then, with some of her most dearly prized historic treasures in ashes, and monuments gone, Paris, scarred and defaced, had quiet at last; and the organization of the third republic proceeded.

The uncertain nature of the republican sentiment existing throughout France at this critical moment is indicated by the character of the Assembly elected by the people. More than two-thirds of the members chosen by France to organize her new republic were ***monarchists!***

The name monarchist at that time comprehended three distinct parties, each with a powerful following, namely:

The LEGITIMISTS, acting in the interest of the direct Bourbon line, represented by the ***Count of Chambord,*** the grandson of Charles X., called by his party ***Henry V.***

The ORLEANISTS, the party desiring the restoration of a limited monarchy, in the person of the ***Count of Paris,*** grandson of Louis Philippe.

The BONAPARTISTS, whose candidate, after the death of the Emperor Louis Napoleon in 1873, was the young ***Prince Imperial,*** son of Napoleon III. [Napoleon II., the Duke of Reichstadt, had died in 1832.]

M. Thiers had not an easy task in harmonizing these various despotic types with each other, nor in harmonizing them all collectively with the republic of which he was chief. He abandoned the attempt in 1873, and Marshal MacMahon, a more pronounced monarchist than he, succeeded to the office of president, with the Due de Broglie at the head of a reactionary ministry. It began to look as if there might be a restoration under some one of the three types mentioned. The Count of Paris generously offered to relinquish his claim in favor of the Count of Chambord (Henry V.), if he would accept the principles of a constitutional monarchy, which that uncompromising Bourbon absolutely refused to do.

In the meantime republican sentiment in France was not dead, nor sleeping. Calamitous experiences had made it cautious. Freedom and anarchy had so often been mistaken for each other, it was learning to move slowly, not by leaps and bounds as heretofore.

Gambetta, the republican leader, once so fiery, had also grown cautious. A patriot and a statesman, he was the one man who seemed to possess the genius required by the conditions and the time, and also the kind of magnetism which would draw together and crystallize the scattered elements of his party.

It was the stimulus imparted by Gambetta which made the government at last republican in fact as well as in name; and as reactionary sentiment increased on the surface, a republican sentiment was all the time gathering in volume and strength below.

The death of the prince imperial, in 1879, in South Africa, was a severe blow to the imperialists, as the Bonapartists were also called, who were now represented by Prince Victor, the son of Prince Napoleon.

Although these rival princes occupied a large place upon the stage, other matters had the attention of the government of France, which moved calmly on. The establishing of a formal protectorate over Algeria belongs to this period.

Ever since the reign of Louis XIV. the hand of France had held Algeria with more or less success. The Grand Monarch determined to rid the Mediterranean of the "Barbary pirates," with which it was infested, and so they were pursued and traced to their lairs in Algiers and Tunis. From this time on attempts were made at intervals to establish a French control over this African colony. During the reign of Louis Philippe the French occupation became more assured, and under the Republic a formal protectorate was declared.

In 1881 Tunis also became a dependency of France; a treaty to that effect being signed bestowing authority upon a resident-general throughout the so-called dominions of the bey.

The fact that in 1878 France participated in the negotiations of the Congress at

Berlin, shows how quickly national wounds heal *at the top!* And further proof that normal conditions were restored, is given by the Universal Exposition, to which Paris bravely invited the world in that same year.

In 1879 M. Grévy succeeded Marshal MacMahon. It was during M. Grévy's administration that England and France combined in a dual financial control over Egypt, in behalf of the interests of the citizens of those two countries who were holders of Egyptian bonds.

But the event of profoundest effect at this period was the death of Gambetta in 1882. The removal of the only man in France whom they feared, was the signal for renewed activity among the monarchists, which found expression in a violent manifesto, immediately issued by Prince Napoleon. This awoke the apparently dormant republican sentiment. After agitated scenes in the Chamber, Prince Napoleon was arrested; and finally, after a prolonged struggle, a decree was issued suspending all the Orleans princes from their military functions.

Almost immediately after this crisis the Count of Chambord (Henry V.) died at Frohsdorf, August, 1883, by which event the Bourbon branch became extinct; and the Legitimists, with their leader gone, united with the Orleanists in supporting the Count of Paris.

A small war with Cochin-China was developed in 1884 out of a diplomatic difficulty, which left France with virtual control over an area of territory, including Annam and Tonquin, in the far East.

In 1885 M. Grévy was re-elected. This was, of course, construed as a vote of approval of the anti-monarchistic tone of the administration. So republicanism grew bolder.

There had been an increased activity among the agents of the monarchist party, which found expression in demonstrations of a very significant character at the time of the marriage of the daughter of the Count of Paris to the Crown Prince of Portugal. The republicans were determined to rid France of this unceasing source of agitation, and their power to carry out so drastic a measure as the one intended is proof of the growth which had been silently going on in their party.

The government was given discretionary power to expel from the country all actual claimants to the throne of France, with their direct heirs.

The Count of Paris and his son, the Duke of Orleans, Prince Napoleon and his son, Prince Victor, were accordingly banished by presidential decree, in June, 1886. And when the Duke of Aumale violently protested, he too was sent into banishment.

In 1887 M. Grévy was compelled to resign, on account of an attempt to shield his son-in-law, who was accused of selling decorations, lucrative appointments, and contracts. M. Sadi-Carnot, the grandson of the Minister of War of the same name, who organized the armies at the revolutionary period, was a republican of integrity and distinction, and was elected by the combined votes of radicals and conservatives.

Another crisis was at hand—a crisis difficult to explain because of the difficulty in understanding it.

The extraordinary popularity of General Boulanger, Minister of War, a military hero who had never held an important command, nor been the hero of a single military exploit, seems to present a subject for students of psychological problems; but his name became the rallying-point for all the malcontents in both parties. A talent for political intrigue in this popular hero made it appear at one time as if he might really be moving on a path leading to a military dictatorship.

The firmness of the government in dealing with what seemed a serious crisis, was followed by the swift collapse of the whole movement, and when Boulanger was summoned before the High Court of Justice upon the charge of inciting a revolution, he fled from the country, and the incident was closed.

In one important respect the Third Republic differs from the two preceding it. A constitution had hitherto been supposed to be the indispensable starting-point in the formation of a government. No country had been so prolific in constitutions as France, which, since 1790, is said to have had no less than seventeen; while England, since her Magna Charta made her free in 1215, had had none at all.

An eloquent and definite statement of the rights of a people once seemed as indispensable to a form of government as a creed to a religious faith. Perhaps the world, as it grows wiser, is less inclined to definite statements upon many subjects! Our own Constitution, probably the most elastic and wisest instrument of the kind ever created, has in a century required sixteen amendments to adapt it to changing conditions.

What is known in France as the Constitution of 1875, is in fact a series of legislative enactments passed within certain periods of time; these, as in England, serving as a substitute for a Constitution framed like our own.

The French may have done wisely in trying the English method of substituting a body of laws, the growth of necessity, for a written constitution. But this system, reached in England through the slowly moving centuries, was adopted in France, not with deliberate purpose at first, but in order to avoid the clashing of opposing views among the group of men in charge of the republic in its inception; men who, while ruling under the name of a republic, really at heart disliked it, and were, in fact, only enduring it as a temporary expedient on the road to something better. And so the republic drifted. There are times when it is well to drift; and in this case it has proved most satisfactory.

Not alone the rulers, but the nation itself, was in doubt as to the sort of government it wanted, or how to attain it after it knew. It was experimenting with that most difficult of arts, the art of governing. An art which England had been centuries in learning, how could France be expected to master in a decade? And when we consider the conditions and the elements with which this inexperience was dealing, the dangerous element at the top and the other dangerous element beneath the surface, the ambitions of the princes, and the volcanic fires in the lowest class; and when we think of the waiting nation, hoping, fearing, expecting so much, with a tremendous war indemnity to be paid, while their hearts were heavy over the loss of two provinces; when we recall all this, we wonder, not that they made mistakes and accomplished so little, but that the government moved on, day by day, step by step, calmly meeting crises from reactionaries or from radicals, until the confidence of the world was won, and the stability of republican France assured.

From 1893 to 1896 was a period of colonial expansion for France. The Kingdom of Dahomey in Africa was proclaimed a French protectorate. Madagascar was subjugated, and in 1895 the Province of Hiang-Hung was ceded by China.

In the year 1894 Sadi-Carnot was assassinated in the streets of Lyons by an anarchist, and M. Faure succeeded to the presidency.

A political alliance between France and Russia was formed at this time. It was also during the presidency of M. Faure that the agitation commenced in consequence of what is known as the ***Affaire Dreyfus.***

Captain Alfred Dreyfus, an Alsatian and an artillery officer upon the general staff, was accused of betraying military secrets to a foreign power (Germany). He was tried by court-martial, convicted, sentenced to be publicly degraded, having all the insignia of rank torn from him, then to suffer perpetual solitary imprisonment on the Isle du Diable, off the coast of French Guiana.

The life of the French Republic was threatened by the profound agitation following this sentence, in which the entire civilized world joined; the impression prevailing that a punishment of almost unparalleled severity was being inflicted upon a man whose guilt had not been proven.

It was the general belief that the bitter enmity of the French army staff was on account of the Semitic origin of the accused officer, and that his being an Alsatian opened an easy path to the accusation of treasonable acts with Germany.

The trial of Captain Dreyfus was conducted with closed doors, and the sentence was rigorously carried out.

As time passed, the agitation became so profound, and the public demand for a revision of the case so imperative, that the French court of appeal finally took the matter under consideration.

The ground upon which this revision was claimed related to an alleged confession and to the authorship of the ***bordereau***, the document which had been instrumental in procuring a conviction. Upon these grounds it was claimed that the judgment pronounced in December, 1894, should be annulled.

The court was compelled to yield, and an order was issued for a second trial—a trial which resulted in revelations so damaging to the heads of the French army that a revolution seemed imminent.

The accused man, wrecked by the five years on the Isle du Diable, again appeared before his accusers in the military court at Rennes. His leading counsel, Labori, was shot while conducting his case, but, as it proved, not fatally. The conduct of the trial was such that the dark secrets of this sinister affair were never brought from their murky depths. And with neither the guilt nor the innocence of the victim proven, the amazing verdict was rendered, "Guilty, with extenuating circumstances."

Such was the verdict of the French military court. That of public opinion was different It was the unanimous belief among other nations that the case against this unfortunate man had completely collapsed. But in order to protect the French army from the disgrace which was inseparable from a vindication of Dreyfus, he must be sacrificed.

The sentence pronounced at the conclusion of the second trial was imprisonment in a French fortress for ten years.

This sentence was remitted by President Loubet; and, with the brand of two convictions and the memory of his "degradation" and of Devil's Island burned deep into his soul, a broken man was sent forth free.

Not the least dramatic incident in this affair was the impassioned championship of M. Zola, the great novelist, who hurled defamatory charges at the court, in the hope of being placed under arrest for libel, and thus be given opportunity to establish facts repressed by the military court. By the French law, the accused must justify his defamatory words, and this was the opportunity sought.

The heroic effort was not in vain. Zola was found guilty and sentenced to a year's imprisonment, which he avoided by going into exile. But light had been thrown upon the *"Affaire."* And he was content.

Upon the sudden death of M. Faure in 1899, Emile Loubet, a lawyer of national reputation, was chosen to succeed him, and his administration commenced while this storm was reaching its final culmination.

With the release of Captain Dreyfus the agitation subsided. But before very long another storm-cloud appeared.

A conflict between clericalism and the Government of France is not a new thing. Indeed, it was at its height as long ago as the thirteenth century, when Philip IV. and Pope Boniface had their little unpleasantness, resulting in Philip's taking the popes into his own keeping at Avignon, and in the issuance of a "Pragmatic Sanction," which defended France from papal encroachments.

The old conflict is still going on, and will continue until the last frail thread uniting Church and State is severed.

The particular contention which agitates France to-day, inaugurated by the late Minister Waldeck-Rousseau, and continued by his successor, M. Combes, had its origin in an act called the "Law of Associations," the purpose of which was to restrict the political power of the Church by means of the suppression of religious orders of men and women upon the soil of France.

This was considered an act of extreme oppression and tyranny on the one side, and as a measure essential to the safety of the republic on the other.

In support of their contention the republican party claimed that the French clergy had always been in alliance with every reactionary movement, and that every agitation and intrigue against the life of the Third Republic had had clericalism as its origin and disturbing cause. Hence, the expulsion of the religious orders was declared to be essential to the safety of the republic.

But the Law of Associations was only preliminary to the real end in view, which was accomplished in December, 1905, when a bill providing for the actual separation of Church and State was passed by the French Senate. There was a time when a measure so revolutionary would have opened the flood-gates of passion, and let loose torrents of invective; and the calmness with which it was debated in the French Parliament makes it manifest that the highest intelligence of the nation had become convinced of its necessity. The bill provides for the transfer to the government of all church properties. This change of ownership necessitated the taking of inventories in the churches, which many simple and devout people, incapable of understanding its political meaning, believed was a religious persecution, and resisted by force. The bill recently passed is aimed not at the Church, but at "Clericalism," a powerful element within the Church, which has been determined to make it a political as well as a spiritual power. With the passage of this bill there no longer exists the opportunity for political and ecclesiastical intrigues, which have made the Church a hatching-ground for aristocratic conspiracies. The severance now accomplished is not complete as with us. Money will still be appropriated from the public treasury for the maintenance of churches in France. But the power derived from the ownership of valuable estates is no longer in the hands of men in sympathy with the enemies of the existing form of government.

Another matter which for a time seemed to threaten the peace of France has been happily adjusted. At an international conference held at Algeciras, for the purpose of considering the demoralized conditions existing in the State of Morocco, France and Germany came so sharply in collision that serious consequences seemed imminent, consequences which might even involve all of Europe.

France, with her territory adjoining the disturbed state, and her long Algerian coast-line to protect, naturally felt that she was entitled to special recognition; while Germany, having invited the conference, claimed a position of leadership.

It was over the special privileges desired by each that the tension between these two states became so acute; and finally the one question before the conference was whether France or Germany should be the custodian of Morocco, insure the safety of its foreign population, have charge of its finances, and be responsible for the policing of its coast. Of course the nation assigned to this duty would hold the predominant influence in North African affairs, and it was this large stake which gave such intensity to the game. The final award was given to France, and Germany, deeply aggrieved but with commendable self-control, has accepted the decision.

The elections recently held in France have afforded an opportunity to discover the sentiment of the nation concerning the policies, radical and almost revolutionary, which have made the concluding days of M. Loubet's incumbency an epoch in the life of France. The result has been an overwhelming vote of approval. In M. Fallières, who has been elected to the presidency, there is found a man even more representative of a new France than was his predecessor. A man of the people, the grandson of a blacksmith, a lawyer by profession, M. Fallières has been identified with every important movement since he was first elected Deputy in 1876; has been eight times Minister; was President of the Senate during the seven years of President Loubet's term of office; and January 17, 1906, was elected to the highest position in the state. The appointment of M. Sarrien, with his well-known sympathies, to the office of Prime Minister, sets at rest any doubt as to the policy initiated by M. Waldeck-Rousseau, and consummated by M. Combes.

With each succeeding administration France has gained in strength and stability, and in the self-control and calmness which make for both. The government and the people have learned that the spasmodic way is not a wise and effectual way.

The monarchist party has disappeared as a serious political factor. There is peace, external and internal. And there is prosperity—that surest guarantee of a continued peace.

One source of the phenomenal prosperity of France in this trying period since 1871 has been her mastery in the art of beauty. Leading the world as she does in this, her art products are sought by every land and every people. The nations must and will have them; and so, with an assured market, her industries prosper, and there is content in the cottage and wealth in the country at large.

What a change from the time less than four decades ago, when, with military pride humbled in the dust, with national pride wounded by the loss of two provinces, and loaded down with an immense war indemnity, the people set about the task of rehabilitation! And in what an incredibly short time the galling debt had been paid, financial prosperity and political strength restored.

For thirty-four years the republic has existed. Communistic fires, always smouldering, have again and again burst forth—demagogues, fanatics, and those creatures for whom there is no place in organized society, whose element is chaos, standing ready to fan the flames of revolt: with Orleanist, Bonapartist, Bourbon, ever on the alert, watching for opportunity to slip in through the open door of revolution.

Phlegmatic Teutons and slow-moving Anglo-Saxons look in bewilderment at a nation which has had seven political revolutions in a hundred years!

But France, complex, mobile, changeful as the sea, in riotous enjoyment of her new-found liberties, casts off a form of government as she would an ill-fitting garment. She knows the value of tranquillity—she had it for one thousand years! The ***people,*** who have only breathed the upper air for a century—the people, who were stifled under feudalism, stamped upon by Valois kings, riveted down by Richelieu, then prodded, outraged, and starved by Bourbons, have become a great nation. Many-sided, resourceful, gifted, it matters not whether they have called the head of their government consul, emperor, king, or president They are a race of freemen, who can never again be enslaved by tyrannous system.

There may be in store for France new revolutions and fresh overturnings. Not anchored, as is England, in an historic past which she reveres, and with a singularly gifted and emotional people who are the sport of the current of the hour, who can predict her future! But whatever that future may be, no American can be indifferent to the fate of a nation to whom we owe so much. Nor can we ever forget that in the hour of our direst extremity, and regardless of cost to herself, she helped us to establish our liberties, and to take our place among the great nations of the earth.

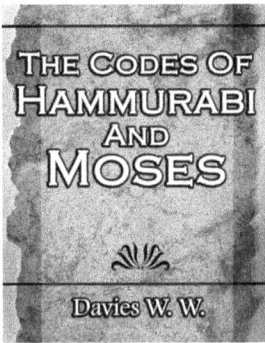

The Codes Of Hammurabi And Moses
W. W. Davies

QTY

The discovery of the Hammurabi Code is one of the greatest achievements of archaeology, and is of paramount interest, not only to the student of the Bible, but also to all those interested in ancient history...

Religion   **ISBN: *1-59462-338-4***

Pages:132
MSRP $12.95

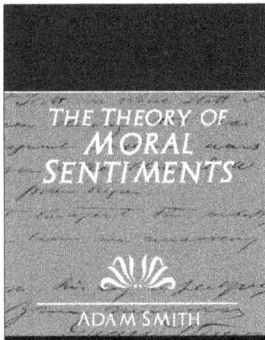

The Theory of Moral Sentiments
Adam Smith

QTY

This work from 1749. contains original theories of conscience amd moral judgment and it is the foundation for systemof morals.

Philosophy **ISBN: *1-59462-777-0***

Pages:536
MSRP $19.95

Jessica's First Prayer
Hesba Stretton

QTY

In a screened and secluded corner of one of the many railway-bridges which span the streets of London there could be seen a few years ago, from five o'clock every morning until half past eight, a tidily set-out coffee-stall, consisting of a trestle and board, upon which stood two large tin cans, with a small fire of charcoal burning under each so as to keep the coffee boiling during the early hours of the morning when the work-people were thronging into the city on their way to their daily toil...

Childrens   **ISBN: *1-59462-373-2***

Pages:84
MSRP $9.95

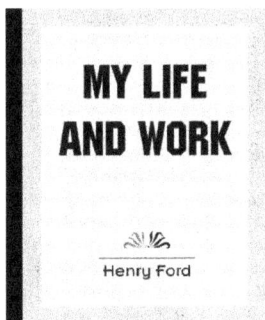

My Life and Work
Henry Ford

QTY

Henry Ford revolutionized the world with his implementation of mass production for the Model T automobile. Gain valuable business insight into his life and work with his own auto-biography... "We have only started on our development of our country we have not as yet, with all our talk of wonderful progress, done more than scratch the surface. The progress has been wonderful enough but..."

Pages:300

Biographies/   **ISBN: *1-59462-198-5***

MSRP $21.95

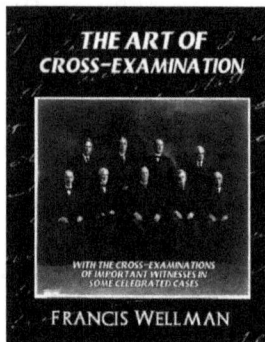

The Art of Cross-Examination
Francis Wellman

QTY

I presume it is the experience of every author, after his first book is published upon an important subject, to be almost overwhelmed with a wealth of ideas and illustrations which could readily have been included in his book, and which to his own mind, at least, seem to make a second edition inevitable. Such certainly was the case with me; and when the first edition had reached its sixth impression in five months, I rejoiced to learn that it seemed to my publishers that the book had met with a sufficiently favorable reception to justify a second and considerably enlarged edition. ..

Pages:412

Reference   ISBN: *1-59462-647-2*   *MSRP $19.95*

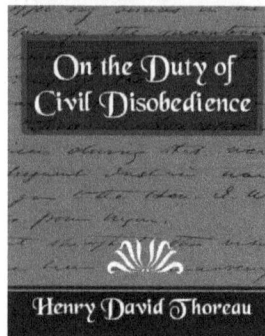

On the Duty of Civil Disobedience
Henry David Thoreau

QTY

Thoreau wrote his famous essay, On the Duty of Civil Disobedience, as a protest against an unjust but popular war and the immoral but popular institution of slave-owning. He did more than write—he declined to pay his taxes, and was hauled off to gaol in consequence. Who can say how much this refusal of his hastened the end of the war and of slavery ?

Law   ISBN: *1-59462-747-9*   **Pages:48**   *MSRP $7.45*

Dream Psychology Psychoanalysis for Beginners
Sigmund Freud

QTY

Sigmund Freud, born Sigismund Schlomo Freud (May 6, 1856 - September 23, 1939), was a Jewish-Austrian neurologist and psychiatrist who co-founded the psychoanalytic school of psychology. Freud is best known for his theories of the unconscious mind, especially involving the mechanism of repression; his redefinition of sexual desire as mobile and directed towards a wide variety of objects; and his therapeutic techniques, especially his understanding of transference in the therapeutic relationship and the presumed value of dreams as sources of insight into unconscious desires.

Pages:196

Psychology   ISBN: *1-59462-905-6*   *MSRP $15.45*

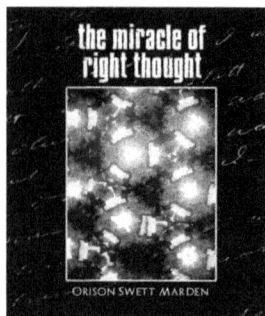

The Miracle of Right Thought
Orison Swett Marden

QTY

Believe with all of your heart that you will do what you were made to do. When the mind has once formed the habit of holding cheerful, happy, prosperous pictures, it will not be easy to form the opposite habit. It does not matter how improbable or how far away this realization may see, or how dark the prospects may be, if we visualize them as best we can, as vividly as possible, hold tenaciously to them and vigorously struggle to attain them, they will gradually become actualized, realized in the life. But a desire, a longing without endeavor, a yearning abandoned or held indifferently will vanish without realization.

Pages:360

Self Help   ISBN: *1-59462-644-8*   *MSRP $25.45*

QTY

The Rosicrucian Cosmo-Conception Mystic Christianity *by Max Heindel* ISBN: 1-59462-188-8 **$38.95**
The Rosicrucian Cosmo-conception is not dogmatic, neither does it appeal to any other authority than the reason of the student. It is: not controversial, but is: sent forth in the, hope that it may help to clear... New Age/Religion Pages 646

Abandonment To Divine Providence *by Jean-Pierre de Caussade* ISBN: 1-59462-228-0 **$25.95**
"The Rev. Jean Pierre de Caussade was one of the most remarkable spiritual writers of the Society of Jesus in France in the 18th Century. His death took place at Toulouse in 1751. His works have gone through many editions and have been republished... Inspirational/Religion Pages 400

Mental Chemistry *by Charles Haanel* ISBN: 1-59462-192-6 **$23.95**
Mental Chemistry allows the change of material conditions by combining and appropriately utilizing the power of the mind. Much like applied chemistry creates something new and unique out of careful combinations of chemicals the mastery of mental chemistry... New Age Pages 354

The Letters of Robert Browning and Elizabeth Barret Barrett 1845-1846 vol II ISBN: 1-59462-193-4 **$35.95**
by Robert Browning and Elizabeth Barrett Biographies Pages 596

Gleanings In Genesis (volume I) *by Arthur W. Pink* ISBN: 1-59462-130-6 **$27.45**
Appropriately has Genesis been termed "the seed plot of the Bible" for in it we have, in germ form, almost all of the great doctrines which are afterwards fully developed in the books of Scripture which follow... Religion/Inspirational Pages 420

The Master Key *by L. W. de Laurence* ISBN: 1-59462-001-6 **$30.95**
In no branch of human knowledge has there been a more lively increase of the spirit of research during the past few years than in the study of Psychology, Concentration and Mental Discipline. The requests for authentic lessons in Thought Control, Mental Discipline and... New Age/Business Pages 422

The Lesser Key Of Solomon Goetia *by L. W. de Laurence* ISBN: 1-59462-092-X **$9.95**
This translation of the first book of the "Lemegton" which is now for the first time made accessible to students of Talismanic Magic was done, after careful collation and edition, from numerous Ancient Manuscripts in Hebrew, Latin, and French... New Age/Occult Pages 92

Rubaiyat Of Omar Khayyam *by Edward Fitzgerald* ISBN:1-59462-332-5 **$13.95**
Edward Fitzgerald, whom the world has already learned, in spite of his own efforts to remain within the shadow of anonymity, to look upon as one of the rarest poets of the century, was born at Bredfield, in Suffolk, on the 31st of March, 1809. He was the third son of John Purcell... Music Pages 172

Ancient Law *by Henry Maine* ISBN: 1-59462-128-4 **$29.95**
The chief object of the following pages is to indicate some of the earliest ideas of mankind, as they are reflected in Ancient Law, and to point out the relation of those ideas to modern thought. Religiom/History Pages 452

Far-Away Stories *by William J. Locke* ISBN: 1-59462-129-2 **$19.45**
"Good wine needs no bush, but a collection of mixed vintages does. And this book is just such a collection. Some of the stories I do not want to remain buried for ever in the museum files of dead magazine-numbers an author's not unpardonable vanity..." Fiction Pages 272

Life of David Crockett *by David Crockett* ISBN: 1-59462-250-7 **$27.45**
"Colonel David Crockett was one of the most remarkable men of the times in which he lived. Born in humble life, but gifted with a strong will, an indomitable courage, and unremitting perseverance... Biographies/New Age Pages 424

Lip-Reading *by Edward Nitchie* ISBN: 1-59462-206-X **$25.95**
Edward B. Nitchie, founder of the New York School for the Hard of Hearing, now the Nitchie School of Lip-Reading, Inc, wrote "LIP-READING Principles and Practice". The development and perfecting of this meritorious work on lip-reading was an undertaking... How-to Pages 400

A Handbook of Suggestive Therapeutics, Applied Hypnotism, Psychic Science ISBN: 1-59462-214-0 **$24.95**
by Henry Munro Health/New Age/Health/Self-help Pages 376

A Doll's House: and Two Other Plays *by Henrik Ibsen* ISBN: 1-59462-112-8 **$19.95**
Henrik Ibsen created this classic when in revolutionary 1848 Rome. Introducing some striking concepts in playwriting for the realist genre, this play has been studied the world over. Fiction/Classics/Plays 308

The Light of Asia *by sir Edwin Arnold* ISBN: 1-59462-204-3 **$13.95**
In this poetic masterpiece, Edwin Arnold describes the life and teachings of Buddha. The man who was to become known as Buddha to the world was born as Prince Gautama of India but he rejected the worldly riches and abandoned the reigns of power when... Religion/History/Biographies Pages 170

The Complete Works of Guy de Maupassant *by Guy de Maupassant* ISBN: 1-59462-157-8 **$16.95**
"For days and days, nights and nights, I had dreamed of that first kiss which was to consecrate our engagement, and I knew not on what spot I should put my lips..." Fiction/Classics Pages 240

The Art of Cross-Examination *by Francis L. Wellman* ISBN: 1-59462-309-0 **$26.95**
Written by a renowned trial lawyer, Wellman imparts his experience and uses case studies to explain how to use psychology to extract desired information through questioning. How-to/Science/Reference Pages 408

Answered or Unanswered? *by Louisa Vaughan* ISBN: 1-59462-248-5 **$10.95**
Miracles of Faith in China Religion Pages 112

The Edinburgh Lectures on Mental Science (1909) *by Thomas* ISBN: 1-59462-008-3 **$11.95**
This book contains the substance of a course of lectures recently given by the writer in the Queen Street Hall, Edinburgh. Its purpose is to indicate the Natural Principles governing the relation between Mental Action and Material Conditions... New Age/Psychology Pages 148

Ayesha *by H. Rider Haggard* ISBN: 1-59462-301-5 **$24.95**
Verily and indeed it is the unexpected that happens! Probably if there was one person upon the earth from whom the Editor of this, and of a certain previous history, did not expect to hear again... Classics Pages 380

Ayala's Angel *by Anthony Trollope* ISBN: 1-59462-352-X **$29.95**
The two girls were both pretty, but Lucy who was twenty-one who supposed to be simple and comparatively unattractive, whereas Ayala was credited, as her Bombwhat romantic name might show, with poetic charm and a taste for romance. Ayala when her father died was nineteen... Fiction Pages 484

The American Commonwealth *by James Bryce* ISBN: 1-59462-286-8 **$34.45**
An interpretation of American democratic political theory. It examines political mechanics and society from the perspective of Scotsman James Bryce Politics Pages 572

Stories of the Pilgrims *by Margaret P. Pumphrey* ISBN: 1-59462-116-0 **$17.95**
This book explores pilgrims religious oppression in England as well as their escape to Holland and eventual crossing to America on the Mayflower, and their early days in New England... History Pages 268

www.bookjungle.com *email: sales@bookjungle.com fax: 630-214-0564 mail: Book Jungle PO Box 2226 Champaign, IL 61825*

QTY

The Fasting Cure *by Sinclair Upton*   ISBN: *1-59462-222-1*   **$13.95**
*In the Cosmopolitan Magazine for May, 1910, and in the Contemporary Review (London) for April, 1910, I published an article dealing with my experi-
ences in fasting. I have written a great many magazine articles, but never one which attracted so much attention... New Age/Self Help/Health Pages 164*

Hebrew Astrology *by Sepharial*   ISBN: *1-59462-308-2*   **$13.45**
*In these days of advanced thinking it is a matter of common observation that we have left many of the old landmarks behind and that we are now pressing
forward to greater heights and to a wider horizon than that which represented the mind-content of our progenitors...   Astrology Pages 144*

Thought Vibration or The Law of Attraction in the Thought World   ISBN: *1-59462-127-6*   **$12.95**
by William Walker Atkinson   *Psychology/Religion Pages 144*

Optimism *by Helen Keller*   ISBN: *1-59462-108-X*   **$15.95**
*Helen Keller was blind, deaf, and mute since 19 months old, yet famously learned how to overcome these handicaps, communicate with the world, and
spread her lectures promoting optimism. An inspiring read for everyone...   Biographies/Inspirational Pages 84*

Sara Crewe *by Frances Burnett*   ISBN: *1-59462-360-0*   **$9.45**
*In the first place, Miss Minchin lived in London. Her home was a large, dull, tall one, in a large, dull square, where all the houses were alike, and all the
sparrows were alike, and where all the door-knockers made the same heavy sound...   Childrens/Classic Pages 88*

The Autobiography of Benjamin Franklin *by Benjamin Franklin*   ISBN: *1-59462-135-7*   **$24.95**
*The Autobiography of Benjamin Franklin has probably been more extensively read than any other American historical work, and no other book of its kind
has had such ups and downs of fortune. Franklin lived for many years in England, where he was agent...   Biographies/History Pages 332*

Name	
Email	
Telephone	
Address	
City, State ZIP	

☐ **Credit Card**   ☐ **Check / Money Order**

Credit Card Number	
Expiration Date	
Signature	

Please Mail to: Book Jungle
                     PO Box 2226
                     Champaign, IL 61825
or Fax to: 630-214-0564

ORDERING INFORMATION
web: *www.bookjungle.com*
email: *sales@bookjungle.com*
fax: *630-214-0564*
mail: *Book Jungle PO Box 2226 Champaign, IL 61825*
or PayPal *to sales@bookjungle.com*

Please contact us for bulk discounts

DIRECT-ORDER TERMS

**20% Discount if You Order
Two or More Books**
Free Domestic Shipping!
Accepted: Master Card, Visa,
Discover, American Express